HOW WE COMMUNICATE
The Most Vital Skill

HOW WE COMMUNICATE

The Most Vital Skill

MARTIN K. BARRACK

Glenbridge Publishing Ltd.
1988

Library of Congress Catalog Card Number: 88-81231
International Standard Book Number: 0-944435-02-5

To Irene, for life.

CONTENTS

No man is an Iland intire of itselfe; every man is a peece of the Continent, a part of the main ... any man's death diminishes me, because I am involved in Mankinde; and therefore never send to know for whom the bell tolls; it tolls for thee.

—John Donne, *Devotions,* 1623

Introduction

People who communicate better command more influence, earn more money, and enjoy more the company of their families, friends, associates, and paramours. Skill in communication is becoming more critical than ever; the sum of human knowledge doubles every decade.

Once, a Leonardo da Vinci or a Thomas Jefferson could master all the science and art of his day. A century ago, we had specialists in medicine called physicians. Today a physician can specialize in allergy, cardiology, dermatology, endocrinology, gastroenterology, gynecology, hematology, laryngology, nephrology, neurology, oncology, ophthalmology, otology, pathology, proctology, radiology, rheumatology, rhinology, or urology, and those are only the ones that rhyme! There are also bariatricians, geriatricians, obstetricians, pediatricians. (Gilbert and Sullivan would have had a field day.) And we still have internists, psychoanalysts, surgeons, and lots more. Among surgeons alone, there are dozens of subspecialists. These people all work on the human body, the same kind you've lived in for decades. Yet usually you can't just go to see a specialist. A physician specializing in general practice, family medicine, or

1

internal medicine has to examine you to decide which specialist you need.

Because human knowledge has grown exponentially, each of us has been forced more and more to address only a very narrow area of human affairs. We depend more and more on others to fill us in. We live by communicating.

For more and more of us, the reduced amount of time for communicating human feelings means that the social communications we do have time for must be much more complex, more subtle, more tightly packed with information, and more accurate. Skill in communication can help support colorful individuality.

Aldous Huxley wrote, "Life is short and information endless," at a time when the sum of human knowledge was about one-tenth what it is today. More than five hundred books on "communication" are now in print.

How We Communicate is an overview. A book aimed at the active reader has to be efficient and concise. This one packs into about 44,000 words—a few hours reading—an integrated perspective on how ideas move from one mind to another. It creates a consciousness of the communication arts with specifics that highlight applications within the reader's own experience.

For the most part, *How We Communicate* addresses areas of practical use to the reader interested in improved academic, business, and social performance. Chapters illuminating a few roads less traveled are included to round out the perspective.

Chapter 1

IN THE BEGINNING

"What's past is prologue." William Shakespeare's words tell us that truth can only be seen from the outside. Many people grew up in the great cities decades ago with few material possessions. But they never knew they were poor; as far as they knew, everyone lived like that. Then, as young adults, they moved out to the suburbs, traveled across the country, and returned to visit their old neighborhoods, seeing the streets and shops more clearly than ever before.

Modern methods of communication are so much a part of our lives that we, like the children of the old neighborhoods, do not readily see them in perspective. The art of communication, now evolving so rapidly, has an ancient lineage. In fact, the story of communication is the story of man. It began a long, long time ago, probably this way:

3

PRIMITIVE COMMUNICATION

In the beginning, the universe was a seminal body no larger than a grain of dust. Perhaps 15 billion years ago, it exploded. For a fleeting instant, all four of the basic forces of nature—gravity, the strong atomic force, the weak atomic force, and electromagnetism—were one. Fiery chunks of rock ripped apart from one another, open space appeared, and gravity became a separate entity. As the universe expanded and cooled, the other forces separated from one another. The strong atomic force inside the nuclei bound protons to neutrons, while the weak force produced radioactive decay. Electromagnetism remained unified with electricity but independent of the other natural forces; it held electrons in orbit about nuclei, bound atoms into molecules and, with massless particles called photons, carried power across vast reaches of empty space. About 10 billion years ago, still in the dawn of Creation, a slowly rotating wisp of gas began to condense, as gravity shaped it into a shrinking ball. The condensation heated the gas, triggering an ongoing fusion of the hydrogen atoms that fueled its steady heat and light.

The new sun threw off a flat disk of gas that condensed to form its planets. Over 4 billion years ago, the gases of the third planet cooled and became a ball of molten rock surrounded by water vapor. With further cooling, a crust formed on its surface, and water rained on the new Earth continuously for about 60,000 years. Three billion years ago, the rain stopped.

Over millions of years, the sun's ultraviolet rays and storms' lightning bolts produced amino acids, formic acid, and urea, which washed into the sea. Eventually, a combination of organic chemicals produced complex molecules that could reproduce themselves. Two billion years ago, these single cells divided into two types: algae and bacteria.

These single-celled organisms reproduced by simple cell division. Asexual organisms were pretty much identical to one another. They could not adapt rapidly to changing conditions, and evolution was very slow. Then a new kind of living being emerged, one that held only half the genetic material it needed to propagate. It had to look for another of its own kind to provide the rest, and it had somehow to indicate its need. On that day, in the primordial sea, the first communication began.

Since every instance of sexual reproduction mixed two sets of genes, each resulting organism was different. As the environment changed, some of the organisms did not make it. Those that did passed on the difference and added variety to the very primitive sexual communication of the Cambrian age.

Until this time, the Earth's atmosphere had consisted of carbon dioxide, water vapor, methane, and ammonia. The sun's ultraviolet rays attacked any animal life that might have evolved on land. But oxygen from algae, over a billion years of time, rose to permeate the upper atmosphere. The ultraviolet rays hammered the oxygen molecules into ozone, and, as a suntan protects its wearer from burning rays, so the ozone layer filtered out most of the ultraviolet light.

The bacteria were also busy evolving. A billion years

ago multi-celled jellyfish, sponges, and worms swam the oceans while oxygen permeated the air. By 500 million years ago the oxygen level stabilized at about 20 percent of the atmosphere, and life appeared on the land.

One of the earliest pioneers was the slime mold, a tiny one-celled organism. When ready to reproduce, the slime mold emitted a chemical that signaled to others nearby. They would crawl to it and fuse together to form a breeding body.

About 400 million years ago, insects touched and pulsated antennae and emitted chemical odors called pheromones; they communicated well enough to run organized little communities. The flying insects, such as crickets and cicadas, advertised for females primarily by sound and gave evening concerts long before humans conceived of similar performances.

Amphibians emerged from the sea about 300 million years ago. The toad, frog, and tree frog males sang love songs in different voices so the respective females could seek them out. The tree frogs contributed further to the evening concerts by singing their mating signals in highly structured, Bachlike trios! When the reptiles arrived some 200 million years ago, they advanced the art of visual or body signals. Lizards bobbed their heads in specific rhythms, did body pushups, and thrashed their tails to mark their territories and, of course, to attract mates. Cobras raised their heads, with hood spread, in the classic warning signal. The great dinosaurs, the brontosaurus, stegosaurus, and tyrannosaurus rex, ruled the hot, dry land and probably used body signals for courtship. The pterodactyls, most smaller but some with wing spans up to twenty-five feet, might have done the same. These great beasts roamed at will, keeping at bay, among other creatures, the synapsids—cold-blooded reptiles with mammal-like skulls and jaws. Then, suddenly, the great dinosaurs disappeared about 65 million years ago, just as the synapsids began evolving into primitive mammals.

Simultaneously, a reptile, archaeopteryx, about the size of a chicken, emerged. It was able to glide through the air and was the ancestor of all birds. As they evolved, birds further developed the art of vocal communication. They expressed joy, fear, loneliness, and sexual desire; they warned of danger, called for help, and proclaimed their territories. Yet, true to their heritage, they depended perhaps even more on body signals, watching one another and making almost imperceptible movements to telegraph their intentions. Some birds also used color as a visual signal; an aggressive robin would turn its red breast directly toward a rival, stretching upward to show the greatest possible area of red.

By 50 million years ago, the synapsids had evolved into mammals in a stunning profusion of shapes and sizes. Mammals, so-called for the "mammae" that provide the young with milk, introduced the integrated use of vocal, olfactory, and tactile signals to extend the range and scope of their communications. A pride of lions, for example, hunted as a team; one discovered the exact location of the prey, another cut off its escape route, and a third drove it toward the ambush site where a fourth killed it. Roles and tactics changed with circumstances; the animals were forced to exchange information and collaborate.

A RADICAL ADVANCE

Animals used vocal sounds, colors, odors, and a myriad of other imaginative techniques to communicate with one another millions of years ago. However, as a general rule they could, and still can, only communicate information about what is going on right then and there. Only one animal species could communicate among its own kind with "displaced reference," the ability to express information about another place or time. They beat us to it by millions of years. Bees executed standard movements in or near the hive, called "bee dances," to tell other bees the locations and strengths of nectar sources.

After a bee found a new source of food, she returned fully loaded to the comb and told the other bees before going back for more. The location of the food was indicated by the rhythm of the dance and the axis of the bee's tail. If the source was near the hive a "round" dance was performed. A "tail wagging" dance indicated that the food was at least three hundred feet away.

The bee measured the distance by the amount of energy she used in traveling from the food source, and expressed it in an inverse relationship to the number of dance cycles in a certain length of time. For example, if the nectar was about three hundred feet away, the bee danced about ten cycles in fifteen seconds. However, if the food source was 30,000 feet away, she only did one cycle in the same fifteen seconds.

The dance even transmitted the precise direction using sunlight and gravity. During her flight to the food source, the bee determined the angle between her line of flight and the sun. Back at the honeycomb, the angle to the vertical at which the bee danced on the vertical face of the comb described the angle between the line of flight to the food source and a line drawn in the direction of the sun. An upward tailwagging run meant: "The flight is toward the sun." A run forty-five degrees to the left meant: "The flight is forty-five degrees to the left of the sun." Honeybees flew at an average of about twelve miles per hour, so a six mile trip took up to thirty minutes. During this time, of course, the position of the sun changed, and the bee changed her dance angle to compensate! If the sun was hidden in the clouds or behind an obstruction, the bee analyzed the pattern of polarized light in the sky. A small opening in the clouds showing even a tiny patch of sky let through a particular angle of polarized light that helped the bee pinpoint the sun's position.

Finally, the scout bee even told her friends how much nectar was waiting. Her dance was much more vigorous and energetic if there was a lot of nectar, or if many flowers a short distance apart had appreciable amounts.

Ever hear the expression, "Make a beeline"? It means to go straight to a destination, and we borrowed it from the bees.

THE DAWN OF MAN

About 40 million years ago, prosimians emerged. These primates lived in the forests and developed flexible front paws to climb trees, swing from branches, and grasp fruit. Life in the treetops also demanded greater alertness, as well as more use of vocal signals for penetrating leaves and branches. The subtle shades of meaning originally made possible by integrating olfactory, tactile, and vocal signals were incorporated into a more extensive system of vocal communication in some of these primate groups. A separate grunt for each idea began to emerge.

Maybe five to eight million years ago, probably in Africa, a primate group came down from the trees and began to spend more time in nearby, open grasslands. Over time, this new group of primates began to walk upright in the tall grasses and to develop enhanced body signals in the form of gestures. Most important, it began to string together separate grunts into modules to express a wider range of ideas.

One million years ago, the most frequent sounds in the forest were the calls of birds and sighing wind in the trees. But the most interesting sounds were the voices of the cave-dwelling, tool-making creatures.

These man-like creatures hunted and killed elephant, rhinoceros, water buffalo, camel, boar, and antelope. To succeed against animals much larger, stronger, and faster than themselves, they had to work together and devise strategy and tactics. To facilitate these tasks, they pioneered an even more radical advance in communication; the separate grunts gradually evolved into words, so that a much larger number of meanings could be developed. Basic conventions for stringing the words together emerged. As they had begun to make primitive material tools, these early men and women also were beginning to use a tool for expressing ideas, a primitive language. Probably a hundred words or so were enough.

Most Neanderthals during the Paleolithic era lived in tiny groups of two or three related families, usually as much as hunting in one area could feed. Ritual burial practices attest to the presence of some religious belief. Each tiny group of cave families spoke its own separate language; even today, among the Australian Aborigines, there are scores of languages spoken by fewer than six people each!

About 35,000 years ago, the bulky Neanderthals were replaced by Cro-Magnons, the first modern humans. As these people explored the deepest recesses of their caves, flickering lights from their burning tapers made moving shadows on the cave walls. Some of the shadows resembled living creatures. Just as some modern urbanites write graffiti on subway walls, Stone Age people learned to communicate their ideas about animals, humans, scenes, or afterlife in a permanent way, as pictures on those cave walls. Some cave pictures were probably used for worship, and some for teaching the young.

Hunters and gatherers do not spend all their time on survival. Perhaps fifteen to twenty hours a week might have sufficed for food, clothing, and shelter, leaving Stone Age people free to think and communicate with those around them. Because their more highly developed brains enabled them to articulate events and ideas in some depth, Cro-Magnons began to combine into small groups and follow leaders who could assure their survival and success. Cro-Magnons' ability to express ideas also helped extend their lives; the oldest had the richest lore, and their ability to communicate it earned them protective reverence long after they ceased being able to hunt animals or collect roots and berries.

Until about 10,000 B.C., food sources had remained fairly constant. Nature had provided humankind with honey, fruits, nuts, tubers, berries, and wild animals. Then a radical development, the "Neolithic Revolution" occurred, and it changed the history of civilization, and communication, forever.

While the men were out hunting game, women discovered how to create food by planting seeds. They reaped golden sheaves of wheat and barley with flint sickles and gathered them in straw baskets. The Bible story of Adam and Eve marks humankind's emergence from Eden, in the fertile crescent near the Nile, Tigris, and Euphrates rivers, into civilization.

Irrigation channels were dug. Oxen were yoked to pull plows. Food was transported and stored in bulk. Many more people could live together. Huts were grouped into villages, then into towns, and finally into the first city-states by about 3500 B.C.

Communication would have to become far more sophisticated to support the more complex and subtle social arrangements of this evolving civilization.

Written communication began to advance. The Sumerians, Abraham among them, settled in what was to become the city of Babylon and used about two thousand pictographic signs to write on clay tablets. "Pictograph" comes from "picture graphics" or picture writing. A picture of a man, followed by a picture of a spear, followed by a picture of a tiger, means "man kills tiger." Over several centuries these pictographs evolved into a wedge-shaped, or cuneiform, writing.

The Sumerians, like the Egyptians, started to write on papyrus instead of clay tablets or walls, and they reduced the number of pictographs in their cuneiform writing to about 550. Later, the cuneiform script changed from the Sumerian horizontal, left to right, to the Semitic vertical, right to left, style. A map of Babylon was drawn. The Egyptians began to set up libraries. Hammurabi, king of Babylon, published the first written code of law about 2100 B.C.

As the Egyptian and Sumerian cultures began to flourish, writers realized that their pictographs were not modular. Each pictograph expressed a complete idea; it could not be divided and recombined, as modules can, to express new ideas. Writers needed a more flexible system to deal with the evolving civilization.

The development of alphabets was gradual. For example, Egyptian picture-writing slowly evolved into symbols for syllables. With creative insight, writers at about 2000 B.C. began to use pictures that mirrored the sounds of the spoken language. For instance, if the spoken language had been English, they might have drawn a picture of a bee followed by that of a leaf, or "bee-leaf," which would have meant belief. The Egyptians called this system hieroglyphics, or "sacred writing," and used it to write *The Book of the Dead,* a collection of religious documents, at about 1800 B.C. Hieroglyphics enabled writers to go beyond the nouns of the old pictographs and represent verbs and adjectives with more versatility.

As the centuries passed, alphabetic systems, which were even more abstract than hieroglyphics, emerged to represent more accurately the sounds of a spoken language. The word "alphabet" comes from the first two letters of the Phoenician alphabet—*aleph,* which meant "ox," and *bet,* which meant "house." The first two letters of the Greek alphabet are "alpha" and "beta." The first two letters of the Hebrew alphabet are "aleph" and "bet."

Moses led the Israelites out of Egypt about 1100 B.C. Scripture records that he received the Ten Commandments on Mt. Sinai and brought his people to Canaan. By 900 B.C. the *Song of Deborah,* later to become part of the *Song of Songs,* appeared. The early Jewish prophets came on the scene about then, and many of the books of the Old Testament, passed on by word of mouth for centuries, were first written in Hebrew during the Babylonian Captivity in the sixth century B.C.

Confucius, Buddha, Lao-tse, the later Jewish prophets, and the major Greek poets, artists, philosophers, and scientists all poured out their creative energy at about the same time, suggesting that some special insight had been communicated around the world about then. The American Indians developed a gesture code expressing concepts such as prayer, rain, clouds, and lightning, describing such objects as arrows, animals, and plants, and addressing human actions and emotions. Their code had adjectives to cover quantity, size, and speed, and could be used for communicating between tribes speaking different languages. By curious coincidence, many of the older Giant Sequoia trees still standing gloriously alive, tall, and beautiful in California also began their lives around the sixth century B.C. In any event, by that time the art of communication among men had advanced enough to convey very sophisticated ideas.

THE ORIGINS OF ENGLISH

In east central Europe, the Indo-Europeans, a single tribe since the New Stone Age, broke apart around 2500 B.C. One group migrated southeast all the way across Europe and Asia to as far as India; the other migrated toward Western Europe. The great distances isolated the tribe fragments from one another, and the language of each evolved separately.

By about 500 B.C., the original Indo-European language had evolved into a dozen different languages including Italic, Germanic, Greek, Celtic, and Slavic. Italic evolved into primitive Latin. Early Latin, in turn, split into Italian, French, Spanish, and several less prominent languages among peasant classes in different parts of Western Europe. The aristocracy continued to speak Latin for several centuries and had the leisure to bring it to the classic beauty we know today.

The Greek offshoot of the Indo-European language evolved into the classic Greek of Periclean Athens. The Celtic branch became Irish, Scots Gaelic, and Welsh. Slavic evolved into Russian and its variants. Germanic began to emerge about the same time as Italic; the Germanic tribes grew and migrated, and their language differentiated into West, North, and East branches. East

Germanic begat Gothic and gradually became extinct. North Germanic, over time, became the Scandinavian languages—Norwegian, Swedish, Danish, and Icelandic. West Germanic split into German-Netherlandic and Anglo-Frisian.

Old English evolved as a dialect of Anglo-Frisian about 300-500 A.D., with the Anglo-Saxon invasions of Britain and the breakup of the Roman Empire. This earliest form is completely unrecognizable to a speaker of present-day English. With the emergence of Northumbrian culture around 500-700 A.D., the Roman alphabet was gradually adopted, and some early Old English literature appeared.

The name "English," by the way, comes from the Angles, the largest and most dispersed of the three tribes then living in England; the other two were the Saxons and the Jutes. Although the modern reader can only understand it after special study, the language is still called "English" because the basic structure and wordstock have survived intact. For example, Beowulf says:

Lif is laene, eal scaeceth, leoht ond lif somod.

It translates: "Life is ephemeral, everything vanishes, light and life together." *Lif* is clearly recognizable. *Eal* is close to "all." *Scaeceth* is "escapes." *Leoht ond lif* is "light and life," and *somod* is "same." The language is twelve centuries old and, like a childhood photo of an old man, hard to recognize.

Around 700-1000 A.D., with the Danish and Norse raids and invasions, the West Saxon dialect began to prevail, influenced by Latin, Old French, and the other Romance languages.

The line of Danish kings in England was abruptly broken by the Norman conquest in 1066. French became the language of the aristocracy, while the common people continued to speak Old English. As the dominance of French speakers in politics, law, and the church hammered the language, it became what we now call Middle English. Geoffrey Chaucer's *Canterbury Tales* appeared about 1387. By that time the decay of feudalism and the Hundred Years War made the London dialect of Middle English the official language.

Today's reader will recognize the general, but not always the precise, meaning of Middle English. For example, from the *Prologue to the Canterbury Tales:*

Ther was also a Nonne, a Prioresse, That of hir smylyng was ful symple and coy. ...

The "great vowel shift," a series of major vowel changes that occurred at about 1350 to 1550, marked the transition to Modern English. For example, the Middle English "hous" (pronounced "hoose") became the Modern English "house." John Donne's *Devotions* of 1623 shows the transition:

No man is an Iland intire of itselfe; every man is a peece of the Continent, a part of the maine . . . any man's death diminishes me, because I am involved in Mankinde; and therefore never send to know for whom the bell tolls; it tolls for thee.

The meaning is now clear to us; we recognize the language as our own.

PRIMITIVE TELECOMMUNICATION

Even in the days when people lived in caves and hunted for food there was a need to communicate over distances. This need was satisfied through prearranged signals. At first, prehistoric man learned to hit hollow logs and trees with a stick. Over milennia, primitive drums were developed, as well as other instruments. Fires were used for smoke signals by day and as beacons by night in ancient China, Egypt, Assyria, and Greece, usually from hilltops.

Longer-range communications were also used, especially in time of war. Aeschylus tells us that, when Troy fell in 1084 B.C., nine beacon fires on nine distant hilltops all in line relayed the news over five hundred miles to Queen Clytemnestra in Argos, Greece! The Bible recounts that Joshua blew a ram's horn to herald the onset of the Battle of Jericho.

The North American Indians, without benefit of a written alphabet and entirely on their own, developed long-range signals, probably thousands of years ago. Along the coasts, they generally used beacon fires at night. These were simple alarm fires used to announce an event, such as the stranding of a whale or the approach of a boat full of strangers. Watchers in the distant village would then prepare for the emergency they expected.

Long-range signals were used most often by the Indians

on open plains and in the southwestern high country and desert lands, where the air is bright and clear. Motion signals were used by these Indians where commanding heights were available. A brave would ride in a circle for a while to indicate "discovery." Then he might execute the specific sign for "buffalo," holding an open blanket at the upper corners and gracefully bringing it down to the ground, suggesting the fall of a large animal. Although this sign specifically referred to buffalo, it was used for any large game. The brave could also execute the "enemy" sign, a confused and rapid riding back and forth, suggesting battle. The discovery sign alone meant that the visitors were friendly. These two signs, "buffalo" and "enemy," were critically important to the tribes.

The Indians also used smoke signals in well-ordered patterns to communicate more detailed messages over greater distances. Fire was set to damp grass or weeds that would burn slowly and emit dense smoke. It was allowed to burn freely for a while until the smoke was likely to have attracted attention. The Indian would then throw his blanket over the smoldering pile and remove it repeatedly, and the specific number, length, and succession of puffs rising to the sky told watchers whether buffalo had been sighted or an enemy discovered, whether they should flee for their lives, come to the rescue, or prepare for war.

Prearranged signals, however, were limited to a very narrow range of information. Most could convey only "yes" or "no." Polybius, the Greek historian, tells us that around 300 B.C. the Greeks came up with a way to encode their twenty-four letter alphabet by placing the letters on a grid of five horizontal rows and five vertical columns, using large, brightly colored vases that could be seen from a distance.

In 1551 an Italian mathematician named Gerolamo Cardano proposed a radical advance in coding. He suggested using five torches on five towers, with all five beacons being either "light" or "dark." The old Greek and Roman signals conveyed each letter in two parts. Cardano, using the dark or "negative" as well as the light or "positive" data bits, eliminated the need for the second part. In so doing, he opened the path for optical telegraphy over two centuries later and foreshadowed the binary concept basic to information management in the twentieth century.

The Greeks had one more contribution to the early world of telecommunication: their word *semaphore*, which means "bearing a sign." The invention of the telescope in 1608 attracted new interest in visual signaling, and the old Greek word was used to describe a French device built for the First Republic in 1794, a series of relay stations spaced three to six miles apart. Each station was a hilltop tower with a little booth for the operators and fixed-mount telescopes directed toward the next tower in each direction. At the top of the tower was a beam with an indicator arm at each end. The beam and arms could assume, in total, forty-nine positions, enough for an alphabet, numeric digits, and some special symbols as well. With good visibility, the French semaphore system could relay three signals, or letters, a minute. A fifty-signal message could be carried from Toulon to Paris, a distance of 420 miles, through 120 towers, in roughly an hour. Mounted couriers would have taken several days. The semaphore gained fame when it was used to relay news of French military victories in August 1794. Within a decade, Russia, Sweden, and Denmark had variations of the French system.

The English were only a year behind. George Murray, an imaginative bishop, built a "shutter telegraph" consisting of six solid shutters, each independently movable, in a three-by-two pattern. By opening and closing various shutters simultaneously, the British Admiralty was also able to communicate over considerable distances.

The United States made the first use of telecommunications in commerce. A Murray line, used primarily by merchants, operated successfully between New York and Philadelphia until 1846. In fact, in 1837 the United States Congress was considering a New York to New Orleans semaphore line when Samuel Morse first showed his working electric telegraph in a New York University lecture hall. As he spoke, all the places called Beacon Hill and Signal Hill in cities and towns throughout the United States began their long, twilight journeys into history.

Chapter 2

"ALL REAL LIVING IS MEETING"

NEW COMBINATIONS

As if it were a distant echo of a time when the forces of nature were one, the Earth's basic design is an attraction of opposites, a mutual dependency, a participation of two or more in major events, a restless series of confrontations creating an endless stream of new combinations. Electrons and protons, the building blocks, attract one another and repel their own kind. The Earth itself has two magnetic poles of opposite charge. It is held in orbit around the sun by an exquisite balance between the centripetal force of the sun's gravity and the centrifugal force of its own mass and velocity.

The animal kingdom depends for survival on the regular congress of opposite sexes. The plant kingdom perpetuates itself by the coming together of male and female substances. And the two kingdoms depend on one another in the great carbon and oxygen cycles that sustain all life on Earth.

22

Interactions are interesting because they produce new combinations, new ideas. A man and woman come together and create a new entity, a "couple." Through their sexual energy they literally create a new human being, complete with its own personality and character. What is most exciting is that the new human being may well be more than either family contributed. Who ever heard of Will Shakespeare's parents? John Shakespeare was a shrewd but illiterate trader, and Mary Arden an attractive but illiterate heiress. Both made a mark in lieu of signing their names but they still gave birth to the crown jewel of English literature!

Communication is fertile when it encourages a new entity to arise, whether it is as simple as a renewed appreciation of sunsets or as intricate as space travel. Such communication makes for a more attractive, healthy environment. Lovers walking barefoot on the beach looking into each other's eyes are enjoying a fertile interaction, unless they crash into a refreshment stand! Teaching a child is fertile because you never know how a child's innate gifts will interact with the heritage of Western civilization to create new ideas. A business conference can be fertile if it has an agenda and a mandate to make decisions.

Conversely, sterile communication results in no new entity. Bickering is sterile. Any communication based on hate is sterile. In fact, sterile communications are negative; by using a creative process for a destructive purpose, they turn creative energy against itself and, having spent the creative energy, end up with less than before. No truly civilized person participates in a sterile communication.

Martin Buber understood. His *I and Thou,* written in the wake of World War I, is a deep and powerful exploration into the nature of God and man. One sentence illuminates its core: "All real living is meeting."

There is a story about a Jewish tailor who had not been to synagogue in several weeks. The rabbi grew concerned and went to visit the tailor. On this chilly day, the tailor had a roaring fire in his fireplace. The rabbi and the tailor looked at each other, neither wishing to begin the discussion. At length, the rabbi took a poker and separated one glowing ash from the others, moving it to the very edge of the firepit. For a while, the separated ash continued to burn brightly. Then, gradually, it began to dim, and before long it was just a lump of carbon. The tailor spoke first. "Rabbi, I understand. I will be in *shul* next Saturday."

ONTOLOGY AND COMMUNICATION

Scientific materialists say the universe is mere physical and chemical activity, that even life and mind are self-continuing chemical reactions. In this philosophically flat universe, a thunderstorm is as alive as an Einstein.

Scientific materialism rose to prominence with Darwin's theory of evolution, which saw a continuum from organic chemicals to man. It advanced with the discovery of DNA, a molecule that contains the code for a replication and translation process accomplished by chemical reactions, reinforcing the continuum between nucleic and amino acids, and ourselves. Mental activity, materialists assert, occurs with electrochemical activity in the brain. Stimulating specific areas of the cerebral cortex can produce specific mental activity.

Similarly, psychologists can often predict the behavior of masses of people. Political scientists do sophisticated polling to predict, within say 3 percent, the candidate for which a supposedly free people will vote. Motivation researchers tell advertisers how to influence people in supermarkets to buy certain products, through cues such as package color and "image." Even background music in many supermarkets is carefully controlled to influence customers' behavior; in the morning, when few customers are in the store, languorous music creates the desire to tarry awhile for there's plenty of time. In the afternoon, as store traffic increases, so does the music tempo, now suggesting the customer move at a faster pace so that all can be accommodated. From this perspective, everything we do is mechanistic.

Most theologians, many philosophers, and some scientists see, instead of a flat universe, a hierarchic one, with the living God at the apex of being, consciousness at the next level, biologic life below that, and physical matter at the base and least real level.

From the hierarchic perspective, information controls the universe; higher levels of information control lower levels, which in turn control chemical and physical activity. For example, there are two separate principles involved in a mechanism. At the base are the fixed laws of chemistry and physics. Superimposed on them are the boundary conditions, defined by information, within which they operate. Metal, glass, and rubber were around a long time before cars, but it was information that shaped and combined them in a way that could be used to transport people.

The carrier of a message must be chemically or physically neutral with respect to the message it carries, or else it could carry only one message. The specific information content of a DNA molecule is superior to the chemical and physical characteristics of its carrier, because it controls them.

If the human race is just a collection of molecules, then ideas are chimerical, and it is vain to communicate them; the paths of glory lead but to the grave. But if information is a higher reality, then communication is a genuine act of creation.

Chapter 3

LANGUAGE

A language is an organized system of expression using widely shared symbols. Some say that any shared system of symbols is a language; computer programmers invariably speak of programming in a language. Others, mindful of the Latin *lingua,* or tongue, from which the word "language" came, feel that only spoken languages qualify.

A natural language arises from and is continually enriched by folk experience; it is ordinarily used in the whole range of day to day transactions among members of a community. An artificial language is one written by a specific person or research team for a narrow purpose.

Every natural language has three main characteristics. The first is its phonetics, or "sound." Even a person who does not know a word of French will instantly recognize its rich, sensuous articulations as distinct from the guttural German. In English and the Romance languages, pitch differences do not distinguish one word from another, but they do in many others including the Scandinavian languages. English and German speakers can handle a whole battery of consonant sounds—"strengths," for instance, has three consonant sounds before and three after a single vowel; most others cannot.

The second main characteristic of a natural language is its grammar, or body of organizing rules. These rules enable a finite number of words to express an infinite range of ideas by specifying the relationship between words in sentences. Some words indicate actions, others tell who is performing them, and still others modify both.

The third feature is semantics, the accumulated experience by which both sounds and rules influence meaning. The word "sleep," for instance, can change its meaning dramatically when followed by "with."

Phonetics, grammar, and semantics are common to all languages. They shape and define the wordstock of every spoken language into a precision instrument for communicating ideas. Schoolchildren decades ago wondered what actually constituted correct phonetics, grammar, and semantics. Our English teacher, Miss Prim, always knew the answer: Correct usage was what she said it was.

Miss Prim, having brought intellectual discipline to generations of boys and girls, has now retired to Florida where she spends her days writing perfect letters to the editor. Her students, now full professors of English literature, hold two opposite viewpoints on correct usage. The populists, liberals all, say that correct usage is what predominates; to communicate efficiently one must use the same codes everyone else does. Most people don't see linguists socially; we talk to business associates, friends, spouses, and lovers. If they understand us, we are satisfied. Finley Peter Dunne's Mr. Dooley made himself clear even, the populists point out, through a green Irish brogue.

The elitists, conservatives to the last, say that a small group of scholars with special knowledge and impeccable taste should set the standard. Ordinary folk can get along with approximations, but someone has to set an absolute standard for those who need absolute precision. No musician would say, "The middle C on my piano is broken but I'll get by with C-sharp." Nor should a writer, say the elitists, have to use dull tools of trade.

Correct usage is somewhere on the continuum between these positions. In more liberal environments, the populist position has more influence, and in more conservative environments, it has less.

Energetic languages support accurate communication by being both efficient and redundant. The artistry of a language to some extent rests on how gracefully it resolves these conflicting requirements.

Efficiency makes it fast. In every major language the words used most often are very short. In English, words of four or fewer letters account for only about 9 percent of the words in an average dictionary but constitute about 57 percent of the average text. In fact, as words become more popular they get shorter. Four decades ago, a few of us watched "television." Now most Americans watch "TV."

Redundancy makes a language accurate. Validation requirements and agreement enable us to trap and correct errors in transmission. The sentence, "She traveled by *tmain*" is likely to be flagged because it violates a validation requirement: No English word begins with *tm*. Then the agreement between "travel" and the mode of travel tells us the word must be *train* and not *tram*. Trams are short distance conveyances; one rides on a tram, but one travels by train. If the sentence were, "She traveled by *plan*," the context would tell whether it should have been "Her travel was planned," or "She traveled by plane."

ENGLISH

At the World's Fair, you can wander about and eat pizza, bulgogi, falafel, paella, sukiyaki, wiener schnitzel, burritos, gyros, or crepes, with apple pie for dessert. Or you can walk around and listen to the languages.

The first language you hear is English. In Shakespeare's day, English was a minor language spoken by a few people on a small island. But by the 1700s, when it began to replace Latin as the language of scholarship, the literate felt they should be able to control, parse, and analyze English as they could Latin. Latin was prized for its formal classic beauty and professional prestige, but it was valued even more because, as a dead language, its meaning remained constant. It was a rosetta stone in whose shadow precise and unchanging code symbols could be formed.

The rules of Latin grammar were superimposed on English, but it was a shotgun marriage, for English had a Germanic base. Nouns, pronouns, verbs, and interjections were defined by meaning, while adjectives, adverbs, and conjunctions were defined by function. Prepositions were defined partly on form and partly on function. This inconsistent grammar violated a basic principle of logic— that you can't add apples and oranges—and so led to confusion. In the expression "a dog's life," the word "dog's" could be either a noun, based on form, or an adjective, based on function! The Latin grammar did improve English as a means of communication, however. In *the slithy toves did gyre and gimble in the wabe,* we know that *toves* and *wabe* are nouns even though we have no idea what they describe. The grammar provides a redundancy check; if the speaker is being imprecise, the listener's own knowledge of grammar will flag it as an error rather than allow acceptance of an error-laden message.

The grammar system also moored the evolving English language to a fixed frame of reference. In our own time, just when interest in formal grammar waned, the mass media took up the job of keeping the various English dialects compatible. If they had not, English would have broken over time into a dozen mutually unintelligible languages.

E Pluribus Unum

A language, like any organism, lives by absorbing vital new words faster than the obsolete ones die away. The word "parlor," for instance, came from the French *parler,* to converse. "Gas" was newly minted from the Greek *chaos* or "formless void." Other new words are knitted together from existing words, like "railroad." With a basic wordstock about half Germanic and half Romance, English has an insouciant way of picking up words from all over. The language has become a magnificent mosaic.

In the time of *Beowulf* and *Roland* every educated Englishman spoke and wrote Latin fluently. In fact, until recently the ability to use Latin freely was the chief mark of a fine education. Physicians wrote prescriptions in Latin and pharmacists interpreted them until just a few decades ago. Many words in the learned fields of divinity, law, philosophy, and science moved directly from Latin to English, among them *affidavit, alibi, animal, bonus, dictum, folio, inertia, innuendo, interim, item, memorandum, recipe, stimulus, vacuum,* and *veto.*

French was the dominant language in England during the Middle Ages. Like a great wave that washes far up onto the beach and deposits objects behind as it recedes, the impact of the French language peaked as its use declined. As the elites began once again to speak English in the 1300s, they continued to use French words of statecraft like *congress, constitution, legislature, president,* and *representative,* ecclesiastical words like *baptism, crucifix, parson, religion,* and *sermon,* and words of the culinary arts such as *broil, fry, grill, roast,* and *toast.* As a rule French terms are more intellectual and abstract than their English counterparts; the French *liberty* is more abstract than the English *freedom,* as the French *probability* is harder to define than the English *likelihood.*

The English mosaic was woven of threads from many

lands. From Spain came *armada, cannibal, galleon, guerrilla, matador, mosquito, tornado,* and *vanilla,* and from Latin America, *canyon, cigar, lasso, mustang, pueblo,* and *rodeo.* From Hebrew came *amen, cherub, hallelujah, kosher, leviathan, manna, messiah, rabbi, sabbath, seraph,* and *shibboleth,* and from Arabic, *alchemy, algebra, alkali, arsenal, assassin, azimuth, cipher, elixir, nadir, sugar, syrup, zenith,* and *zero.*

The Irish offered *blarney, bog, brogue, clan, galore, hooligan, shamrock, slogan,* and *whiskey;* the Russians *balalaika, mammoth, tundra,* and *vodka.* From the other side of the world, Hindi pitched in with *chit, cushy, dungaree, guru, gymkhana, juggernaut, jungle, loot, nabob, pajamas, punch* (the drink), *pundit, shampoo,* and *thug,* while Persian contributed *bazaar, caravan, catamaran, chess, divan, lilac, paradise, salamander, shawl,* and *taffeta.* The Japanese donated *banzai, hara-kiri, karate, samurai,* and *tsunami.* And the list goes on forever. Even Aboriginal Australian got in with *boomerang* and *kangaroo.*

English picked up still more vigor from the tribes native to American soil. The Algonquins alone gave us *caribou, hominy, mackinaw, squash,* and *toboggan.* Above all, Amerindians named places all over the land, from Manhattan to the Mojave Desert.

American ethnic groups added their own color and strength, from the Yiddish *chutzpah* and *schlock* to the Sicilian *capo* and the Latin *macho* to the black *right on.* And the language is still changing. New words are born every day; others die. "Astronaut," "empower," "modem," and "telework" come in while "croon" and "grifter" go out.

Some words reflect the humor of people who coined them long ago. "Tart," as a noun, is defined as a small open pie with a sweet filling and also as a woman whose charms are available commercially.

The Great Pronoun War

As Miss Prim explained it, the pronoun "his" is in some cases gender neutral. "Every executive has his attaché case" was used even when some executives were female, because English has no other gender neutral, singular pronoun and because everyone understood the idea being communicated.

In the 1960s many career women noticed that this usage made the masculine pronoun superior to the feminine, because it could encompass both genders while the feminine pronoun could not, subtly suggesting that the masculine gender was the only one needed. These career women recalled the line in *The King and I* where the king tells Anna that a bee must go from flower to flower, but a flower never goes from bee to bee!

Grammarians have split four ways on this issue. Some defend "his" as short and traditional, although inconsistent with social trends. Others opt for "his or her" as correct although cumbersome. A third group uses "their," retaining brevity but substituting inconsistency between singular and plural for inconsistency with social trends. A fourth prefers "s/he." No consensus has emerged yet; stay tuned!

Snapshot of a Word During Birth

When terminals were first connected to remote mainframe computers through telephone lines, the industry coined the phrase "on-line" to indicate that the terminal was at that moment connected to the computer.

In the mid-1980s, when public information utilities became popular, researchers noticed that they could not search databases for the word "on-line." The computer search programs interpreted the hyphen as a space and saw it as "on line."

These mainframe programs could only search for one word at a time, and "on line" was two words. They could search for two words adjacent to one another with an appropriate command such as "onADJline." But "on" is not a searchable word; it is on a list along with other common words like "the," "and," and so on, that are ignored because they would unduly tie up computer time without being useful. The programs could search the word "line," which is not on the restricted list, and get a torrent of references every time, few useful.

So database researchers, miffed that they could not run searches on a major concept of their own profession, began spelling it "online." The new spelling is spreading rapidly and will soon find its way into one dictionary after another.

English Around the World

English has three distinctive characteristics. First, it

has relatively few inflections, or variable words. For example, the word "ride" has five forms: "ride, rides, rode, riding, ridden." Its German equivalent, *reiten*, has sixteen. English adjectives have practically no inflections at all.

Second, English has unusually flexible word functions; the same word can serve as either a verb or a noun. We can "plan" our next move or we can have the builder draw a "plan." Most other languages do not have this capacity because they use different endings for verbs and nouns.

And third, English has an exceptionally open vocabulary, accepting words from other languages or creating compounds and derivatives at will.

In these three respects, especially in its open word functions and vocabulary, the English language reflects the American character. Saul K. Padover, in his book, *The Genius of America,* wrote:

> It has been said that America's most original contribution to political theory has been to have no theory. In a special sense, this is true. American political thought is an aggregation of concepts, phrases, slogans, creeds, shibboleths, and traditions that has never been ... distilled into symmetrical theoretical architecture.

English is the *de facto* international language. It is the national language of twelve nations with 350 million people: the United States, Canada (with French), Bahamas, Barbados, Grenada, Jamaica, Trinidad and

Tobago, Guyana, England, Ireland (with Gaelic), Australia, and New Zealand.

American English is spoken on every continent. Like the land from which it sprang, its motto could be *e pluribus unum,* "Out of many, one!" In our own land as in every other, English takes on regional flavor and characteristics. From the New York dialect, made "standard" by the television networks, south to the Cajun dialect of the Louisiana bayous and to the Tex-Mex of the Lone Star State, and west to the "far out" California variety, we could paraphrase Woody Guthrie, "This language was made for you and me."

In Britain, the abbreviation RP, for Received Pronunciation, denotes the London elite speech of Cambridge and Oxford as conveyed through Eton, Harrow, Rugby, Winchester, and the BBC. Its sharp contrast with the working class London cockney was highlighted in the musical *My Fair Lady.* The British retain some quaint grammatical differences; collective nouns, for instance, such as *government* and *committee* take singular verbs in the United States but plural verbs in England. And, of course, they cling to such terms as *lift* for "elevator" and *torch* for "flashlight."

The idioms, too, are different. In England, for instance, when a fellow arranges a date with a girl, he might say, "I'll knock you up Saturday afternoon at one o'clock," intending to knock on her door at the appointed hour. If the girl were American, however, she might receive a different impression.

In Australia and New Zealand, the language reflects

the informal but energetic character of its early British settlers, who often had to find words for flora and fauna unlike any they had known before. Cattle so intractable that only roping could control them were "ropable," and the term then came to mean very angry. To "barrack," or jeer noisily, recalled the Irish *barrack* meaning to brag or boast. But some of Australia's English came from the aborigines. A "corroborree," for instance, was originally a warlike aboriginal dance, but then became any large, noisy gathering.

In India, English is the only means of communication between the central government in New Delhi and the populations that speak languages other than Hindi, most of which utterly seal their speakers off from contact with the international trade community. English is disdained by many in India as a reminder of the country's pre-Ghandi days and also as a "Christian" language, but it is still widely used in business, science, and higher education as a matter of simple necessity.

Africa uses English in somewhat the same way. Although it has scores of tribal languages, English is an official or semi-official language of administration in most African countries. As always, the most vigorous local expressions propagate; the South African *trek* and *commando* are now in worldwide use.

English today is the international language *par excellence.* It is the medium for 80 percent of the information stored in the world's computers.

IN OTHER WORDS

Americans live in a country so broad and dynamic that many rarely stop to think of, let alone engage in, languages other than English. Not so for those who came before us, nor for Europeans who can often reach several different language enclaves within a few hours drive, nor for the Japanese who depend for their livelihood on commerce with the United States and Europe. We can learn from other languages, however; each language is a mirror reflecting its cultural heritage, as well as being an efficient means of communication within a special environment.

The American Indian Languages

The origins of the languages spoken by the native North Americans are shrouded in the mists of time. Although they are descended from people who crossed the Bering Strait during the last ice age about 35,000 years ago, their languages have little in common with any spoken in Asia. The Spanish, French, and Italian explorers of several hundred years ago left traces of their own words in a number of the Indian languages. As the pioneers pushed westward in the early 1800s, many Indians became bilingual, and their languages picked up a few English words.

There were once as many as three hundred different languages in North America. Probably half that number of languages survive today, some spoken by only one or two ancient members of a tribe. These languages are spoken on the reservations primarily by the older and more traditional people. Their children are less interested in the old ways. Although a few native American languages like Navajo are growing in strength, most remain in decline.

The Romance Languages

The Romance languages are so called because they echo the Latin of the Roman Empire, not love in the Tuileries! They seem musical because they emphasize their clear, bell-like vowels rather than their consonants. They sound fast because individual words are stressed lightly and often elided. The intonation patterns tend to amplify and reinforce a speaker's emotional excitement.

French is the most important of the Romance languages because of its use in international diplomacy, its matchless grace and beauty, and its major contribution to English. But whereas English is a free enterprise proposition, the French take a statist approach to their language; the French Academy is a group of scholar-police who enforce vigorously the precise rules bequeathed by grammarians in the 1600s and 1700s.

Enforcement is accomplished through government edicts about what is correct on school and college examinations as well as on entrance examinations for teaching and government positions. State-owned television stations use only the approved style. As a result, educated French is very formal and complex, in vivid contrast to the casual speech of the working classes. However, in France the working classes envy the educated style, while United States workers disdain similarly formal American English as pretentious and stuffy.

The French Academy watches over the fast-changing French vocabulary to assure its continued Gallic character. This effort is not just to stamp out words like *le parking* or *le drugstore.* The French Academy has been watching new computer manuals, for instance, to be certain that only pure French words, rather than anglicisms, are used. It is thus more difficult for French computer engineers to learn the specialized English of their trade so they can read the American technical journals in order that the beauty and purity of their language will be preserved.

President Mitterand's High Commission on the French Language is also vigilant. Through subordinate bodies, it is hard at work devising new terms, supervising the words used by newspapers and television stations, and prodding executives into trying French first when dealing with foreigners! The Computer Terminology Commission, for instance, has come up with *le logiciel* for software. Data processing has become *l'informatique.* Some of their creations are clever; random access memory, for instance, is *mémoire vive* while read only memory is *mémoire morte.* Others exist to be different even at the price of confusion; the official French term for "disk drive" is *tournedisque,* which so resembles the French word for "phonograph" that *le disk drive* is smuggled in whenever possible.

Curiously, the French word for "computer" came from a quintessentially American company. When IBM began to sell computers in France around 1960, it wanted a French-sounding word to describe the product. Rather than go with "computer," which implied a stream of calculating operations, IBM played to the French linguistic sense with the term *ordinateur,* from the Latin "putting in order." Consequently, two decades later, the original IBM PC was described in France as IBM l'OP, for *ordinateur personnel.*

The French take all this seriously; it is possible in France to sue someone for using non-French words like *le weekend.* A few socialist deputies feel this law does not go far enough, however. Some years ago, they called for a law making such usage a crime, prompting the newspaper *Le Monde* to suggest wryly that the widely used term *sandwich* be rendered: *deux morceaux de pain avec quelque chose au milieu* (two pieces of bread with something in the middle).

Ironically, these very strict rules of grammar take French further from Latin than any of the other Romance languages, and it is consistent with the traditional French sense of independence that the differences apparently were not caused by outside influences. French culture also shows up in the areas of special excellence in the language. As English is the language of business and science because Americans do more business and science than anyone else, so French has more richness and verisimilitude than any other in the arts, and in the making of wine, cheese, and love.

Spanish is important because it is the official language not only of Spain but of all Latin America except Brazil. In the United States, there are large parts of Miami, Los Angeles, El Paso, and many other cities where Spanish is used more than English. Standard Spanish is the

Castilian dialect spoken in Madrid. Latin America follows Castilian grammar, while using a more musical pronunciation as well as more English words. Spanish is also the most efficient of the major Romance languages; it is relatively direct, clear, and free of oddities. As a result, it has retained its core structure even among remote peasants in Central and South America.

Italian is important more as a vehicle of culture than for the number or economic clout of its speakers. It is the senior vernacular of the Roman Catholic Church, as well as the language of Dante, Machiavelli, and many of the world's finest operas. There are more speakers of Portuguese, for instance, but they have had less impact on Western civilization.

Standard Italian is the language of Rome and is closer overall to Latin than any of the other Romance languages. In effect, it is "more Romance," probably for two reasons. First, the Catholic Church has both sustained the Latin tradition and permeated every nook and cranny of Italian life. Second, the Italian ethos is deeply imbued with reverence for a glorious past; in language, Latin is the glorious past.

German

German is the official language of Germany and Austria and the most prominent of Switzerland's four official languages. As an offshoot of old West Germanic, it is closer to English than any of the Romance languages.

For example, *Gott* is "God," *Mutter* is "mother," *Vater*

is "father," *innen* is "inside," and the list goes on and on. German often compounds words; during World War II everyone knew the *Wehrmacht* was the "war-maker," or army. In Vienna, the *Stattsoper* was the "state's opera" or grand opera, while the *Volksoper* was the "folks' opera" or light opera. German even borrowed from us and compounded a two word phrase that came out *Studentendemonstration!* The American at a *Festhaus* who is told *Guten Appetit* will appreciate the kind wish and begin to eat. If she hears that a *Hund* is chasing a *Katze* who in turn is chasing a *Maus,* she will probably understand and look around. Those capital letters in the middle of the sentence, by the way, mark nouns. Germans want to be very sure you know what the subject is. The verbs, adjectives, and everything else you will just have to find for yourself.

Japanese

Japanese is important as the language of over 120 million industrious people. Its ancient and intricate heritage bred a babel of dialects until radio and television spread the Tokyo dialect over all the islands as a standard.

A majority of Japanese words are native, and most of the rest are of Chinese origin. All the words beginning with "p" are either onomatopoeic or adopted from European languages. Also, very few native Japanese words end in a nasal sound. For that reason, some companies introducing high-tech products coin names starting with "p" or ending in a nasal sound to suggest that they are new or foreign! Many Japanese words depend on pitch for meaning; in Tokyo, *hashi* with a high-low pitch pattern means "chopsticks," but with a low-high pattern it means "bridge." The Japanese do not stress individual syllables of a word, though, so the effect is metronomic and musical.

Japanese can be written in any of three separate alphabet forms. Traditional written Japanese consists of *Kanji*, oriental pictographs each representing an entire word. There are more than 20,000 *Kanji*, of which about 2,300 are in frequent use. Like the old Egyptian and Sumerian pictographs, they limit the range of ideas that can be expressed, since each requires a separate symbol. *Kanji* especially resist ideas from outside the traditional culture, since entirely new symbols are then required. This may account somewhat for the traditional purity of Japanese culture. *Kanji* read fast because each symbol is iconic, a "picture" of a concept, like the international road sign symbols.

Two Japanese alphabets, like English, use letters; they are far more flexible but require an extra step to reach intuitive recognition. *Hiragana* are used especially for literary works. *Katakana* are used primarily for business correspondence by computer and typewriter and also for foreign loan words and onomatopoeic words.

Esperanto

One good language is not heard much at the World's Fair. Esperanto is not a natural language. Written over a century ago to improve worldwide communication and understanding, it is extremely regular and predictable.

Vowels are sounded as in "c*a*r," "m*e*n," "mach*i*ne," "f*o*r," "t*u*ne." Nouns end in "o," as in *arbo* (tree). Adjectives end in "a," as in *bona* (good). Plurals are formed by adding "j" to a noun and its adjective; *bona arbo* becomes *bonaj arboj.*

Words are formed by adding modifiers to root words. *Mal* denotes the opposite, so *malbona* would be "bad." Intensity is added by "eg" so *bonega* is "very good."

The regularity of Esperanto proves a key to understanding the nature of language itself. Students of English who search for a rule of pronunciation covering "bough," "cough," "dough," "rough," and "through" are often so immersed in learning special cases that they can lose sight of the structure.

Esperanto is spoken today only by a tiny band of enthusiasts, for it is not a mirror reflecting a cultural heritage; it did not rise organically from the experience of a people. A plastic jug is superior in some practical ways to a beautiful ceramic urn. This manufactured, plastic language is an interesting curio, but no Shelley will ever write a classic ode to a plastic urn!

LANGUAGE BARRIERS

Some years ago an American official went to France on business. He had been given precise walking directions from his hotel to the United States Embassy, Building D, at 58 bis rue de la Boétie. Upon arriving at 58 rue de la Boétie, however, he found not an embassy but a very French bank. With only a few words of French vaguely recalled from college days, the official looked at the directions that had been crystal clear up to that point, then at the bank, then at the street name, then at the passing Parisians.

Seeing a doorman at a nearby building, he tried, "Où est l'ambassade des Etats-Unis?" The doorman replied, "Place de la Concorde." This answer did not fit the directions given him in English by a man who knew the area well. The American, puzzled to his bones, decided to trust the directions given in his own language and replied, "Pardon, monsieur. L'ambassade des Etats-Unis est au 58 rue de la Boétie." The doorman looked at him carefully, as one looks at a strange creature. "Place de la Concorde," he repeated, indicating that it was about two miles to the west. The American showed him the directions written in English. The doorman shrugged and took a guidebook from his pocket. His finger pointed to a street map on which the ambassade des Etats-Unis was shown as being at the place de la Concorde. He said once more, "Place de la Concorde."

The American considered walking to the Concorde and asking for help but decided against it. Too far. He started to walk back to 58 rue de la Boétie and suddenly noticed a public telephone. Aha, he had the embassy's phone number! He entered the booth, then realized he had no idea how to operate the phone or what coin to use. Now what? He decided he'd have to find someone who could speak English. Fortunately he was on rue Faubourg St. Honore, Paris's counterpart to New York's Fifth Avenue, so he began walking from one elegant store to the next asking, "Parlez-vous anglais? Parlez-vous un peu d'anglais?" Eventually, a shopkeeper spoke the best words the American had heard so far that day. "Yes, I speak English. How may I help you?" He explained how to use the public telephone and selected two 20-centime coins from the American's pocket change, saying, "Use these."

The American official phoned the embassy and asked the secretary who answered where on Earth they were. The secretary replied, "58 bis rue de la Boétie." "But I was there," the American protested. "There's only a bank." The secretary replied, "Yes, sir, the bank is at 58 rue de la Boétie. We are at 58 *bis.* Go to the end of the bank building, walk through the alley, and you'll see the United States flag and Marine guard. Didn't you know that *bis* in an address means 'next to'?"

It's true, every word. *Bis* had been carefully specified as part of the address, but the American official had disregarded it; after all, the United States Embassy in Paris must be pretty big and would stand out once one was in the general area. And it is a prominent compound, directly across the street from the statue of Marie Antoinette on the place de la Concorde, with its own statue of Benjamin Franklin in front, and back then it had a small annex called "Building D" about two miles to the east on rue de la Boétie!

The American official was competent. In English he could find any place efficiently, but the difference in languages made him a caricature in the eyes of the Parisian doorman. Millions of Hispanics, Southeast Asians, and other minorities live in the United States today without speaking English. Many of them are intelligent and competent, but their images are refracted into caricatures by the language barrier.

America is a nation of immigrants. Most of us, or our parents or grandparents, came from somewhere else. When our parents or grandparents arrived in the new world, the first thing they did was try to learn English as fast as they could. Some never could get the hang of it, but they worked and scrubbed and pushed so that their children could learn English. And in so doing, the farsighted people of the fading photographs brought a second meaning to the motto *e pluribus unum.*

As we expand our systems of communication in this country, we might reflect that they depend on a core of common language. We need to assure that every permanent resident of this great land can speak its one language. Only then will it be open. Only then will all the libraries and books and magazines and newspapers, the television and radio sets, the telephone lines, microwave towers, satellites, cellular radio systems, and all the rest be acolytes to the American dream.

At the same time, however, we need to communicate accurately across language barriers. Many of us need to be able to read publications written in French, German, Spanish, Japanese, Russian, and Chinese as well as in English. Computer programs are available to translate directly from one language to another, but they are extremely challenging to write because of the subtleties of each language. Additionally, as the number of essential languages increases, the number of translation programs increases as the square of that number minus one. For instance, the ability to translate a document in any of these seven languages into any other requires forty-eight programs. Add one more language and you need sixty-three. When we were told to go forth and multiply, this was not explained!

A proven approach could solve the translation problem. Old Ben Franklin, architect of the United States postal system, knew that if his minions tried to carry mail from each house or firm to every other they would make far too many trips. So he resorted to the hub concept. Like the spokes of a wheel, his carriers brought mail from each location to a hub, or central office. There the mail would be sorted. Once the sorting was completed, each mail carrier returned to his local area and delivered it. If a letter had to go out of town, the central office routed the mail to a special long distance "pony express" rider who would carry it to a central office in the distant city. There it would be routed to the local area to which the letter was addressed.

This hub concept, as seminal an idea as the wheel itself, was used exactly the same way centuries later. Old Ma Bell figured out a long time ago that she couldn't wire every home to every other home, so she set up a central office in every community and wired each home to it. Hubs are used everywhere to distribute information over a large population.

The hub concept is probably the way to go for most translations. Esperanto could be the key; its rational, consistent structure, simple and regular grammar, and cultural neutrality make it ideal for computer interface. Just sixteen programs could translate between eight languages through Esperanto.

Even with the best translation programs, however, language is still organic, the pride and province of the human race. Some years ago, as an experiment, the common English aphorism, "Out of sight, out of mind," was translated by a computer from English into Russian, then back into English. The computer printed, "Invisible idiot."

LANGUAGE AND REALITY

Many of us try to inflate our images by inflating the language. Physicians speak of "modalities" of treatment, an inflation of "modes," or "methods." Educators are famous for the latest in afflatus; "cognition" is usually used in place of "learning." Lawyers use rigid, redundant terminology; a "tortious breach," for instance, is a broken promise. Inflated words sound dull and lifeless. We all do it sometimes—ever use "bodily," as in "bodily fluids," instead of "body"?

Coined words should clarify or enhance the art of communication. "Laser" was needed to describe the new device that produced coherent light; such words add precision to the language. Others, like "zap," add vigor. The genuine words ring like fine Waterford crystal.

Linguistics is the science of language. Traditionally it has been rigorous, austere, and aloof. In the 1960s and 1970s it embraced MIT professor Noam Chomsky's concept of "transformational grammar," which disregarded real spoken language and pursued an idealized form believed to exist in the mind of each participant in a conversation, an echo of Plato's world of forms.

Linguistics in the 1980s has become more practical, more interested in real communication. Georgetown University Professor Deborah Tannen, in *That's Not What I Meant!*, describes the changes in pitch, loudness, pacing, tone of voice, and intonation, as well as the devices such as questions, storytelling, and ambiguity, that are as much a part of the message as the words.

Probably the most interesting and controversial issue in linguistics is male and female language use. Anthropologists Daniel Maltz and Ruth Borker assert that the different ways men and women communicate originate in childhood. Little girls often share secrets with a best friend; their talk is private and intimate. Little boys, by contrast, often play in groups; their talk is open and competitive. As they grow up, women continue to express intimate thoughts more fluently than men do, while men, as Betty Lehan Harrigan points out, are more comfortable in teamwork argot.

Professor Tannen cites as an example the man and woman riding home in a car. The woman asks, "Are you thirsty?" The man answers "No," and they ride on. The woman is miffed; she had expected a counterquestion, "Would *you* like to stop?" This question would have led to a negotiation wherein they could explore one another's level of interest in a rest stop. The man had heard a straight request for information and provided it, whereas the woman expected him to evince interest in her by asking about her needs. Professor Gregory Bateson calls signaling by the nature of one's response the "metamessage" level of conversation.

Our perceptions are influenced by language and

innuendo in the public as well as in the private environment. Ideas are shaped by words. Phrases in the daily newspaper can affect our idea of what is being reported. For instance, the terrorist "claimed credit" for the bombing. This phrase in every other context indicates a proud achievement, as in "The doctor claimed credit." Criminals "admit guilt."

A tendency to break the link between cause and effect is showing up more often in American media as an attribution of responsibility to an inanimate object. "The car went out of control," often replaces "The driver lost control." Innuendo is used to smuggle in ideas that are not allowed through the front door. When reporting on Nicaragua, for instance, liberals refer to the "progressive Sandinista government," while conservatives, noting that Augusto Sandino was a pluralist and social democrat, refer instead to the "Soviet-backed regime." Liberals describe the rebels as "contras," meaning the opposition. Conservatives describe them as "freedom fighters."

Resolving legal issues under our adversary trial system means that two sides describe the same facts from opposite perspectives. Each side inevitably uses words and grammar to convey its perspective to the jury.

Prosecutors in a rape trial use direct, vivid words with aggressive overtones to establish an atmosphere of violence. Defense attorneys, on the other hand, use romantic words to suggest consent and rely on abstract language to diminish emotional responses. The prosecutor will say, "He tried twice ... ," while the defense attorney will say, "After two unsuccessful attempts ..." During abortion trials, the prosecutor will say "baby" or "child" and "smother" or "suffocate." The defense attorney prefers "fetus" and "terminate," or "dilation and curettage." Grammar counts, too. Prosecutors generally use the "active voice," as in, "We believe ..." Defense attorneys more often use the passive "It is believed ..." Prosecutors often use the definite article, "Did you see *the* baseball bat?" The defense prefers the indefinite, "Did you see *a* baseball bat?" Even judges use grammar for effect; they refer to themselves in the third person as "the court" to convey Olympian neutrality.

Language manipulation is often used in politics to promote public approval of programs the public does not love. In the 1930s an unemployed person was said to be "on the dole." After a while, the dole fell into such disrepute that the name was changed. It was called "relief" to imply a sense of being temporary and of being rescued from starvation.

A few years later people began to associate "relief" with disrepute, so the name was changed to "welfare." The term was right out of the Constitution's "promote the general welfare" clause; who could oppose it? After a while, though, people began to see "welfare" as disreputable.

The term "human resources" was then coined to show that these recipients are not a drag on society but instead a resource. Along with it came "human services." "Human services" is a classic. Chosen to suggest that the poor are after all human, the term is currently used as a surrogate for "poor people's." The Department of Health and Human Services does not consider even the promotion of good health a "human" service; if it did, the words "Health and" would have been deleted from the name.

Who would so debauch our means of communication? Pogo said it: "We have met the enemy and he is us!"

Chapter 4

FACE TO FACE

Face to face communication is the best medium when decisions based on the message will be of paramount importance. The most critical challenge to a person's communication skills comes during the interview with St. Peter at the Pearly Gates. St. Peter opens the big book, turns to a particular page, reads it a moment, looks up and says, "Tell me why you deserve to come in." Try it right now: Stand up, close your eyes, and tell St. Peter why you deserve to come in!

Another critical challenge is the job interview. It determines where and how well a person will live, whether she will be happy in her career, perhaps who her friends and companions will be, and what the future will bring. In an hour, more or less, the applicant has to convince an interviewer that she would be a better choice than any of the other applicants with similar credentials. She has to create a little army of signals marching in lockstep: eyes, hair, face, clothing, body movements, words—all precisely aligned. In fact, the interview begins the moment

56

the applicant and interviewer set eyes on one another. The interviewer notices the applicant's clothing in the first instant. As the applicant looks around the room for a fleeting moment, moves toward the indicated chair, and sits down, the interviewer observes manner, bearing, and confidence. In some circumstances, the assessment phase of the interview might actually be over before either person has uttered a word.

Users of public information utility forums, as well as amateur radio operators who use digital techniques, depend entirely on the message text for information. There is no accent, no inflection by which the other person's race, age, education, or professional level can be inferred. An absence of cues makes for an intriguing conversation as long as the exchange of ideas is simple. It works fine for casual chitchat about jobs or world affairs, but when a message becomes more complex, as many business or sexual messages are, it becomes necessary to convey it through several channels at once so the recipient can weave the many messages into one. The place in which the message is given, the clothing worn by the person giving the message, the vocal inflections, and even the facial expression and physical movements convey information. Only by processing all of this information can a person be sure the message has been properly understood. As an example, consider this scenario:

Early one morning on Manhattan's Park Avenue a young woman stepped into a waiting taxi. The sun shone in the cabbie's eyes as he drove east on the Expressway and then south on the Van Wyck to JFK Airport.

At the airport, the woman checked her suitcase and carried her attaché case onto the aircraft. Five and a half hours later the big 767 passed low over the San Diego Freeway and landed in Los Angeles.

Her cab made a right turn into Century City and stopped in front of a prominent hotel. She stepped out and checked in. In her room, she took a small, expensive laptop computer from her attaché case and went to work.

The next morning, after a room service breakfast, she took the elevator to a small conference room she had rented and met with two men. They talked for three hours. They then went to lunch and talked for two more. At two o'clock, they smiled, shook hands, and went their separate ways. She went immediately to her room and typed a series of agreed-upon specifications into the small computer. Then she telephoned her office and used its built-in modem to transmit the specifications immediately.

Early the next morning the woman's cab drove south under the four stacker to the airport exit. Once on the 767 she sank into her first class seat and gratefully accepted copies of *Business Week* and *U.S. News.* The evening sun shone in a cabbie's eyes as he drove her toward the Queens Midtown Tunnel and home.

The trip had cost her company two thousand dollars. She could have had a teleconference for two hundred. What did her company get for its money and two days of her time? It got nonverbal behavior patterns. Popularly called "body language," more accurately "body signals," these nonverbal communications added a constant stream of information to what the voices alone conveyed. They were worth her trip.

OUR HIGH SPEED TRANSCEIVERS

The eyes have it! All the information you could want, delivered so fast that an instant's inattention could miss an important signal. Bright sparkling eyes, half-closed bedroom eyes, mournful eyes, steely eyes, and glassy eyes all tell a story. These versatile and efficient instruments of communication both transmit and receive information at very high speeds. During a two-party face to face conversation, each person usually looks straight at the other about 40 to 50 percent of the time. Less than about 30 percent suggests that someone has something to hide. More than 60 percent suggests more interest in the other person than in what is being said. Moreover, eye pupils become wider when one sees something pleasant. As always, context counts; if lights are low, the pupils will also dilate.

In fine restaurants, visual conversation with waiters is an art. The subtle diner can call the waiter, ask for coffee, or signal for the check using eyes in combination with small brow or head motions. Customs inspectors often rely on eye signals; hundreds of times every day they ask travelers what they have to declare and then assess, within a few seconds, whether the answer is truthful. They know the look of relaxed innocence, they recognize the fleeting instant of fear and the effort at camouflage.

The Spanish philosopher José Ortega y Gasset, in *Man*

and People, said that every look tells us what goes on inside the person who gives it. He spoke of "the look" as something that comes directly from within "with the straight line accuracy of a bullet." The eye, he wrote, is "a whole theater with its stage and actors" in its range of expression. Ortega was fascinated in particular by "bedroom eyes," the look the French call *les yeux en coulisse.* The lids are almost three quarters closed and appear to be hiding the look, but they actually compress it and "shoot it out like an arrow." "It is the look," Ortega wrote, "of eyes that are, as it were, asleep but which behind the cloud of sweet drowsiness are utterly awake. Anyone who has such a look possesses a treasure."

Eye contact is usually the first communication that occurs between a man and a woman. Our Latin American neighbors have a folkway that depends entirely on it for introductions. Each Sunday morning in the *plaza,* or town square, the single men walk casually around the square in one direction; the single women walk in the opposite direction. A young man will signal his interest in a young woman by eye contact. The type of eye contact reflects his character and personality; a shy glance, for instance, might suggest modesty. If the woman reciprocates with her eyes, they both have a few minutes to consider whether to carry it further and exchange a few words. This ritual of the *paseo* is a gentle and civilized way of meeting the opposite sex.

In the game of men and women, there are some interesting eye rules. In the United States, a man may look at a woman for only one or two seconds unless she gives him permission to continue, such as with a returned look and a smile. A woman may look at a man longer only if she is willing to engage in conversation with him; a longer look is a signal to approach.

Lord Byron knew the power of eyes to intrigue the opposite sex. He had seen the beautiful Lady Wilmot Horton at Lady Sitwell's ball. Although still in mourning, Lady Horton wore a brightly spangled dress, one that drew attention to her attractive figure. But his poem did not reflect her figure:

> She walks in Beauty, like the night
> Of cloudless climes and starry skies;
> And all that's best of dark and bright
> Meet in her aspect and her eyes.

A HELPING HAND

In *Kismet* the Poet sang of the marvelous expressiveness of hands. He listed many uses, especially in storytelling, but in truth they communicate far more than even his impassioned song could tell. We have extensive gesture systems for greeting, for vehicle traffic control, for airplane pilots on the ground and in the air, for control of baseball players on the field, and more. We have gesture signals for music; Leopold Stokowski, in his Philadelphia Orchestra years, conducted in near darkness, without baton, a spotlight only on his magnificent hands.

Some hand signals are widely used. The upraised thumb, for instance, signals either general approval or interest in a ride. The upraised third finger, on the other hand, connotes disapproval.

Even the most common greeting gesture of all can convey both a basic message and overtones. A brief, firm handshake says, "We are business associates who can work together." A firm handshake that lasts a little longer says, "We should get to know one another better." A gentle touch with only incident movement can express emotional support or sexual interest. A powerful handshake says, "Me Tarzan!" Many women subconsciously signal affection with their hands. They rarely show their palms in ordinary situations, for the "back of the hand" signals indifference. When courting a man, however, they "palm" at every opportunity. Female politicians sometimes "palm" their audiences.

The most highly developed hand signals are used in the modern manual communication system. It is primarily used by persons who live in a world of silence, but it offers advantages to anyone who takes the time to become proficient. Social gatherings offer a case in point. Adept spouses can communicate across a room discreetly. Because manual expression is sometimes partly readable even by the uninstructed, it can signal interest to an intriguing member of the opposite sex. And when the band turns up its amplifiers all the way for a rendition of "When the Saints Go Marching In," it might be the only way to converse!

There are even more reasons to learn manual communication. In a business meeting, representatives of an organization can quietly signal assent or warning to one another, and the other side will probably be unable to "read" the signal. Of course, the adept executive will be able to read the other side's signals without their realizing it. In noisy industrial environments, workers trained in manual communication might be able to save time by using their hands. On the New York subways, it's either manual communication or a newspaper. Travelers in Moscow could use manual communication in wired hotel rooms; it's a lot faster than writing on a long yellow pad. Scuba divers can discreetly proposition one another below the surface. And, of course, it's all you get at Gallaudet!

Experienced signers use formal sign language, finger spelling and pantomime in concert. A formal sign language is a system of symbols formed by the hands to represent complete words. Usually, one sign equals one word. The most highly developed are American Sign Language, British Sign Language, Danish Sign Language, and Japanese Sign Language. They are quite different from one another, as all are from the American Indian sign language; in fact, a signer fluent in American Sign Language might be unable to comprehend any of the others. An international sign language called Gestuno has been invented; however, it lacks the social and community roots that give any language vigor and flair. Like a plastic rose beside a real one, it has only the appearance of life and, like Esperanto, is used only by a tiny band of adepts.

American Sign Language, usually shortened to "ASL" or "Ameslan," is a system of signs that represent English words as they are used in the United States. Although the basic structure of ASL was invented, it has expanded through use by gifted signers, just as spoken English is expanded and enriched by gifted speakers and writers.

ASL is partly iconic. An icon is a symbol resembling

the object it represents. For instance, "house" is signed in ASL by two flat hands raised in a "steeple" position and then drawn back to form a roof. "Eat" is represented by touching the fingers to the lips. "Apple" is signed by holding an imaginary apple as though biting into it. Iconic signs, given slowly, are sometimes intelligible to nonsigners. Many signs, though, are not iconic. The ASL sign for "America" is horizontal interlinked fingers of both hands, which could represent the stripes of the American flag or the union of the states into a federation.

Iconic signs are the visual counterparts of onomato-poeic words. An onomatopoeic word is one that sounds like the thing it represents. We represent a dog's bark, for instance, as "bow-wow" or "woof woof" and a bell as "ding-dong." Iconic signs vary from one formal sign language to another in the same way onomatopoeic words do; for instance, the French represent a dog's bark as *woah woah,* and the Chinese, as *wang wang.* The Germans represent a bell as *bim bam.*

Signs that appear iconic in isolation are often unrecognizable to a nonsigner when they appear in conversation, partly because of the fast rate of signing but also because the signs appear blended together when made by experienced signers. The same thing happens to a person learning Spanish.

Finger spelling is used when there is no available sign for a particular concept, or when the signer wants to convey an exact word rather than a general concept. It is regarded as a separate signing mode for convenience.

Pantomime imitates objects and events as they occur

in nature, just as an artist paints a scene before him. It is a true universal, as anyone privileged to have watched Marcel Marceau on stage knows. Pantomime is not part of ASL, but it is used extensively because it adds variety and color to a sign conversation. It conveys intensity especially well—signing "I am happy" conveys only that, but a thousand-watt smile says it all.

Some scholars question whether it is possible to make as many fine distinctions in the visual mode as in the acoustic mode. At present, spoken languages offer more richness and depth; signed languages tend to be literal and direct. But there is no inherent characteristic of the visual mode that makes it any more narrow than the acoustic mode. Formal sign language is young. When it begins to transfer meaning, as spoken languages do with idioms, and to compound signs as German compounds words, the poetry and power of signed languages will rise to the heights commanded by their spoken counterparts.

ON THE MOVE

Historically, the most highly developed body signals have been reserved for hunting and mating. Today we have replaced the hunter's loincloth and spear with the three piece suit and market research. The mating ritual includes everything from want ads ("WSM into TLC seeks WSF for discreet relationship") to computers ("Which of the following is most important to you?"). But body signals, after 200 million years, are still potent communication symbols. They are a major reason for that trip to the coast.

One man walks into an office without knocking. He marches straight to the client's desk, shakes hands immediately and sits right down. Another knocks and waits for a response; on entering, he walks only a short distance toward the desk and stops to await a further invitation.

The walk toward the desk conveys time frame. A brisk walk suggests that the person entering is important, has a lot to do, and wants to be brief. The person who ambles from door to desk may stay a while.

Sometimes a business situation calls for "stroking" another person to get approval for a plan. When the opposite sex is involved the usual ingratiating signals— sitting foward in the chair, giving a broad smile, and brightening the eyes, for instance—can be misinterpreted. We clarify by introducing nonsexual signals. This clarification must be done at the outset; a person trying to figure out whether the sideshow is a come-on will not pay attention to the intended message. A friendly but businesslike tone of voice, casual mention of one's spouse or significant other, or fondling a wedding ring will do.

Body signals are highly developed symbols. They transmit messages without commitment. A woman, for instance, sees a handsome man at a party and signals interest by looking at him and smiling. They begin a conversation, but she soon realizes they are mismatched. She begins to "play with" a ring he had not noticed before and to look around as if for another man. The man soon departs. Without body signals, she might not have been willing to take a chance and open what might have been a beautiful, even lifelong, relationship. Once involved, she would have had to say, "You are pleasant, but we have little in common. If this conversation continues, I will not have time to seek someone more in tune with my interests. I would like to do so; please excuse me."

Many signals are common to both sexes. Preening gestures, for instance, are often used by both men and women. A woman might briefly check her appearance in a compact mirror, while a man will finger his tie or lapels. Either might briefly touch the lips with the tongue. On the other hand, a person whose arms or legs are crossed is, often, symbolically putting a bar across the road, although some people are merely finding a comfortable position or are chilly. If both arms and legs are crossed, the probability is greater that the person is trying, consciously or not, to signal "no." Overall body position is usually a signal. At a party, for instance, if a seated woman angles her body toward the man she is talking with, she is probably enjoying the conversation. If, even while she is looking straight at him, her body is angled toward another man in the room or toward the door, she might be wishing she were somewhere else. Similar body signals usually suggest compatible people. If a man and a woman tend to copy one another's body movements then they are probably getting along well. But if each changes position to avoid their being in similar positions, storm clouds are in the air. If one copies while the other changes to escape the copy, the one escaping is apt to dominate the relationship.

All these signals can provide vital information. But remember: Just as a single word does not a story make, neither does a single body signal communicate much useful information. "The voice is Jacob's voice, but the hands are the hands of Esau." As redundancy—the repetition and variety of signals—increases, so does the reliability of the overall impression.

Some body signals are transmitted directly by a person's physical structure. Tall men are seen as natural leaders; as children they had enough physical strength to be dominant, and they took that pattern with them into their adult years. Broad-faced people of both sexes project more self-confidence than narrow-faced people; perhaps they see their own images in the mirror while grooming, assume that their characters are reflected in their faces, and act accordingly. Hawk-nosed people are seen as tough, shrewd, "hard-nosed" business managers. People with full lips seem relaxed and expansive, while their thin-lipped associates are viewed as precise, methodical, and taciturn.

Although many individuals do not match these stereotypes, enough really do to etch a subconscious association into many people. The person who wants to communicate an opposite message is sailing into the wind, and should consistently use a wide range of signals to overcome the image.

Elegance can turn an adverse physical characteristic to positive advantage. During the Illinois Senate race in 1858, Abraham Lincoln was once accused of being two-faced. He might have responded in kind, but the gangling, homely Lincoln instead turned to the attending crowd and said, "I leave it to my audience. If I had another face, would I wear this one?"

WEARING THE MESSAGE

Clothing is a means of communication that does not have to be carefully controlled during a face to face meeting. The handshake, eye contact, tone of voice, table manners, and the rest are practiced "on stage"; the less skilled practitioner must divert some attention from the business at hand to their graceful execution. Clothing is selected and put on ahead of time. With a diligent investment of time and energy, a person can send clear signals even while otherwise preoccupied.

Broadly, clothing communicates the first and most prominent message. Most managers, professionals, and other upper middle-income types meet a great many people with whom they do not work regularly. These people are sized up by their clothing, their body carriage, and little else. In the course of time relationships shift, and a person might have to impress someone she has not much considered before. The cumulative effect of being dressed either with exquisite taste or run of the mill haste will be strong.

In some cases, clothing tells a story in detail. Military uniforms overtly convey branch of service, rank, specific organization, achievement record, and even overseas experience. The practiced observer also notes whether the shirt and slacks are starched and sharply creased, whether the shoulder patch is affixed precisely in the prescribed position with invisible stitching, and whether the shoes are polished like black mirrors.

Civilian clothes are less overtly descriptive but convey very specific impressions. Priests and judges wear black robes that conceal their body contours as much as possible to suggest disembodied intellect. They thereby encourage ordinary persons in their presence to obey them as if they were the higher authority they represent.

When a man wears a black suit in the office, he subconsciously reminds those around him of society's most revered figures and thereby participates in their authority. Most business suits are "cool" colors because executives want to signal that they are rational and reliable. A gray suit, lacking any chromatic color, suggests objective neutrality. A blue suit subconsciously suggests "true blue" integrity. As always, there are exceptions. Funeral directors wear black to convey respect for the departed. Country singer Johnny Cash performed in black for many years to remind his audiences that people who live at subsistence levels are human beings and not ciphers. But it is these very exceptions that give nonverbal communication its power. Nonverbal communication allows plausible deniability; ask a powerful executive in a black suit whether he is trying to assert power and he will say, "Who me? Heavens no. My tailor said this suit would make me look slimmer. Do you think it does?" even as he resolves to transfer the asker to the company's Death Valley office.

Dressing for social occasions engages the same codes of association in an opposite way. At a party or social gathering, most people would rather be liked than respected and would rather appear sexy than disembodied. The clothes that suggest relaxed self-confidence, sexuality, or country good-old-boy will broadcast their silent signals to all present.

The strength of a message can be part of the message itself. A message that is too powerful can boomerang. For instance, standard business strategy includes dressing for the job you want, not the job you have, to signal the decision makers that you fit in with the target environment. Occasionally, a clerk will wear a very expensive three-piece suit, trying to broadcast the message that he is ready to move up. The suit would be fine in the executive suite but not in the management trainee job he covets. The gap between what he is and what he is trying to signal is too wide; the signal received by the decision makers is that the lad is eager but not ready.

A business message expressing understated elegance can be sent through accessories. The attaché case, especially an expensive brown leather one, is a perennial winner; it might carry nothing more than some impressive papers back and forth and a sandwich every morning, but the signal is still transmitted. Executive pen sets, expensive watches, and top grade shoes and socks are nearly subliminal in most situations; people generally will not remember individual accessories, but they will receive and retain the message that this person has class.

THE MESSAGE SCENT

A scent is actually an airborne army of molecules. These volatile little molecules jump into the air from their source and ride tiny currents. A very few of them drift high into a person's nose where special cells detect their specific characteristics and notify the brain.

Animals have always used organic chemicals to communicate. Female moths release bombykol, a single molecule of which will excite and attract a male moth miles away. Fish use chemical signals to identify individual members of a species; a dominant catfish has a particular odor recognized by other catfish. These communicating odors are pheromones, organic chemicals that elicit a specific behavior. They carry messages only between members of the same species, and are often perceived subconsciously; the receiver is not aware of a message.

We humans have traditionally believed that, at the summit of evolution, we have cast off so primitive a technique. Even when a hound tracks a man in shoes across open ground walked by dozens of others, we notice the hound rather than the message scent. But human beings communicate naturally through pheromones. For instance, women who live or work together tend to menstruate about the same time of month; apparently each woman emits pheromones that carry body signals to the others.

Of course, not all human odor signals depend on pheromones or other natural odors. Perfume carries semiconscious scent messages. Usually, the professional woman at the office wears a fresh, clean scent that suggests feminine wholesomeness and perhaps sharpness and clarity. In a romantic environment, the perfume, and its message, are exactly the opposite; a musky, sexual scent reminisces of liaisons past and hints of those to come. Colognes worn by men, too, tell a story. Men communicate less among themselves by subconscious odors. Women are more apt to notice a man's scent signals, especially if he is wearing the cologne *she* gave him last Christmas eve!

AN ENVIRONMENTAL IMPACT STATEMENT

An office, inn, or home is a means of communication that does not have to be carefully controlled during a face to face meeting. It can be precisely calibrated to broadcast a message to all who enter, and it can facilitate other avenues of face to face communication. Real estate people talk about location, location, and location. They are thinking of offices, hotels and restaurants, and homes.

The Office

The first fact about an office in a large organization is its physical location. If it is on the same floor as the executive office, it telegraphs to the cognoscenti that you have arrived. It means you are visible to the corporate grand panjandrums and have an opportunity to impact their thinking.

Once on the right floor, the office with more power is the one nearest the Chief Executive Officer. Same game, next level. If the CEO is impressed with you and needs somebody for a high-visibility assignment, he or she can beckon without having to get other concurrences. Corner offices, with windows in two directions, are also "power" offices because they are a smaller reflection of the CEO's office, even though the CEO has a better view.

If the location telegraphs power level, the interior furnishings telegraph status. Stacks of papers, some aging, say "Better hang on to this in case someone asks for it." Paper clutter signals low status, because its owner is too cowed to say he can't provide a document he once had some connection with, and because it speaks of poor records management. The neat desk says, "I am in control here." The office's accoutrements tell the visitor more about a person's status than the most garrulous water-cooler gossips. Carpets, couches, carafes, credenzas, and comfortable chairs are working tools of the person who meets and deals with important people.

Personal memorabilia are a small art form in themselves. Most of them say, "I think about my home life while I am at work." A few items, however, are positive. One is a modest color photo of the family; it suggests stability and, in some situations, neutralizes sex signals. Another is anything that confers glory, say a Bronze Star, a sports trophy cup, or a graduate diploma.

Less Formal Places

Americans usually go to a party for good conversation. Elites, who communicate more effectively than most people, often go to several parties a week. The peripatetic partygoer understands, "I drink to make my friends amusing." In France and Italy, by contrast, outdoor cafes serve as an environment for good conversation. A glass of Pouilly Fume Lin or even Perrier can get the ideas flowing.

To experience an extraordinary environment for face

to face communication, one must go to a great hotel. Communication is the primary purpose of grand hostelry. Any good motel will offer an attractive room and bath, a decent meal nearby, and basic recreation. But captains of industry who watch the bottom line the way a hawk watches its prey don't often hold conventions at the average rest stop; they go for a great hotel.

Look first in the lobby. The great hotels have sound-absorbing environments. Big overstuffed chairs, the kind you can sit in for hours, visually attractive but unobtrusive walls, floors, and ceilings, as well as small amenities erase, insofar as possible, a guest's need to attend the mundane. The guest does not have to move back and forth to find a comfortable seated position; the chair accommodates. The guest does not have to endure loud sounds, remain hungry, search long for a restroom, or do anything else. The guest is free to concentrate on other things.

Now go into the restaurant. Again, the dining area will be impressive, but it will never distract. The servers are efficient, but discreet. A business meeting in this environment is rarely casual; often people who will be participating in a formal conference later are sizing one another up, building coalitions, testing ideas. They are listening to one another's words, watching one another's eyes and other body signals, and formulating responses. Menus in elegant restaurants are usually conventional, because an entree that diverts attention to itself is counterproductive. And so the great hotels offer the "cattleman's cut" or the "captain's platter"; everyone orders with confidence and moves on to the business at hand.

WE ARE WHAT WE EAT

In the high-stakes games of business and sex, lunch is a theater of operations. Eating is only one of many things to do while lunching. As in every game, there are rules. They vary from one city to another, especially in the power cities such as New York, Washington, D.C., and Los Angeles, and from level to level; lunchers at the White House operate differently from those at the Holiday Inn. But some general principles apply.

First, lunching with a boss, a competitor, or even a particular sales representative can be a signal. The person you're lunching with might be signaling, too. Brightly lit restaurants are places to signal other business players; signals only work if seen! Of course, if the objective is sex in the afternoon, then low lights and a corner booth signal discretion; your partner will appreciate it. Second, allowing someone worth lunching with to be visibly kept waiting signals disrespect. Third, the top players won't risk their afternoon clarity; a three-martini lunch says *poseur.* President Carter tried to make war on this little institution and the little institution won; there are a lot of poseurs. Fourth, the first hour is foreplay, the second is business. Paperwork at the table is staff stuff; major league players are more concerned with people decisions than with details. Fifth, eating after everyone else stops signals gluttony; skip dessert. Sixth, picking up the check graciously but immediately and firmly signals responsibility.

All the world's a stage, quoth the bard, and diners with a date or business associate are merely players.

Shall we have a drink before dinner? A wine or whiskey, carefully selected by brand and vintage or age, ordered somewhat casually, suggests an easy familiarity with the finer refreshments and, in combination with other signals, can send a mature, aged-in-the-wood overtone. Mixed drinks vary, but most have less cachet.

Healthy food is in fashion, so a salad is usually in good taste. Aristotle's golden mean is alive and well, so moderation is in; munching on several rolls signals inability to wait for pleasures yet to come.

The main dish can send a whole symphony of signals. Above all, it should be within one's capacity for graceful dining. Cumbersome food—lobster for instance—eaten expertly and discreetly can signal elegance; eaten clumsily, the same meal can be as negative as dousing a burger and fries with ketchup. Simple foods, such as broiled fish, can signal health consciousness, but in some environments they also signal a minimalist philosophy. A good steak, on the other hand, can imply a sensual personality.

Desserts can be skipped altogether to suggest either health awareness or asceticism. A fresh fruit dessert usually implies health. A really fancy dessert is devil-may-care, suggesting gluttony or that one lives for the present with little interest in the future.

These are only a few basic signals. They can be reinforced, modified, or cancelled by the choice of restaurant, personal clothing and carriage, and conversation.

North Americans and Europeans often entertain business associates with dinner at home. When they do, they are apt to show their guests around the house, sometimes even taking them into the boudoir and showing them the master bath. This symbolically conveys an openness and warmth, an "I have no secrets from you" sense, even as a handshake symbolically conveys, "I have no weapons." The Japanese are more private; they rarely entertain at home. When they do, it is invariably in a room designed for the purpose; it has a bath nearby, and the guest is expected to remain in that area for the duration of the visit.

North American and European restaurants offer menus, so that each guest can select the dishes of his choice. In many restaurants, the menu embraces a "choosing ritual"; the printed menu might be very large in size, or on polished wood, or elaborate.

The Chinese restaurant takes a middle position. Its printed menu is rich in variety but physically less prominent, and food arrives in dishes that encourage sharing. When "house dinners" are ordered, the idea of who ordered what is submerged. *Dim sum,* a wide variety of small treats brought to guests every so often, also encourages sharing.

The traditional Japanese restaurant, with its hibachi cuisine in which food is prepared on a grill around which diners are seated, takes sharing all the way. Host and guests alike often eat the same dinner, symbolizing shared values. The saki ritual is the epitome of Japanese dining; everyone pours for someone else. The cups are exceptionally small and must be filled often, so each diner must continually look after the well-being of those seated nearby.

We communicate through eating. A child who grows up with the saki ritual embedded in his or her cultural heritage will carry its values into adult professional life, family life, and generations to come.

Chapter 5

THE TELEPHONE

The telephone concentrates human emotion. As in *les yeux en coulisse,* the entire message is narrowed and directed through a single channel carrying information, attitude, and voice. Effective telephone users work all three; they array their information, project a positive, dynamic attitude, and train their voices to sound natural and clear.

The voice answering a phone call makes a tremendous difference, for it operates during the protocol phase when both parties are trying to establish the "character" of the call. A secretary who answers with a bright, cheery, businesslike introduction will establish a bright, cheery, businesslike call that is both productive and pleasant.

Business telephone use is an art form. The ploys for getting through resistant secretaries, for instance, are legion. Some callers use the First Name Ploy: "Hi, this is Marty. Is George in?" Others prefer the Important Ploy: "This is Marty at Headquarters. Put George on, please!"

Still others favor the Odd Hours Ploy, calling early or after hours, when the manager might answer the phone directly. Proficient users often ask the secretary's name the first time they call, and then say hello by name each time after that.

Efficient executives array beforehand all the information they'll need, so they can see it during the conversation. If a pitch is needed, they'll script it in advance so they sound competent and use the fewest possible words. The efficient executive's attitude is polished to a gleam. A sense of quiet enthusiasm and drive comes straight through the wire. Voice quality is cultivated. Words are clear, with pauses to let the other party respond. Pace is slow when emphasizing major points, fast when summarizing.

The efficient executive uses state of the art telephone technology to increase operating efficiency. If a third party could clarify a point, the efficient executive uses "three-way calling" so the third party can join the conversation immediately. If a consensus of all the regional managers is needed, the efficient executive sets up a conference call and addresses the situation at once. The efficient executive usually has a car telephone to make productive use of time on the road.

THE TELEPHONE NETWORK

In 1865 the *Boston Post* gave its august opinion: "Well informed people know it is impossible to transmit the voice over wires, and that, were it possible to do so, the thing would be of no practical value whatsoever."

Today, the telephone network and the information it carries at nearly the speed of light reach into every house and work place in the land.

When you make a call from your house, you see only the telephone instrument, provided by an "equipment" company. A second company, called an "operating company" or "telco," provides dial tone and local service. A third company, called a "carrier," carries your long distance call from one state to another.

Your telephone generates tones and an electrical analog of your voice. These go over a pair of wires that are entirely your own all the way to the nearest hub, or central office. When you pay each month for a "line," you are literally renting that pair of wires from the local telephone operating company.

When the tones get into the central office, they control one or more switches. If the call is to a friend on the next block, the first switch it encounters will connect your pair of wires directly with hers. But suppose you want to call a friend in the next town. Then the central office switches your call onto one of the phone company's own "trunk" circuits that go from the central office near you to the central office near him. His central office will then switch the call onto his pair of wires.

The adventure starts when you call a relative three thousand miles away. Your local central routes the call to a specially equipped office, where it is switched onto a long distance network. There, the signal travels underground in the big cities, sometimes in the form of light racing through tiny glass tubes. As it gets into open country, your voice travels on wires draped over the familiar tall, wooden poles. When it gets to the mountains, your voice is routed into a microwave transmission tower where it becomes a narrow, precisely aimed radio signal passing over areas completely inaccessible except by snowmobile eight months a year. It goes back onto the wires again to another specially equipped office, from there to the local telco central office near the relative, and onto her pair of wires.

The international call has a more striking adventure. In most cases, your call goes to a "dish" antenna that beams it skyward. It goes 22,335 miles up to a satellite, high enough that an observer sitting on it would see the Earth as a great, blue-and-white globe with deep black space surrounding it. The satellite is in geosynchronous orbit; it revolves around the Earth at the same speed at which the Earth rotates on its own axis, thereby appearing to be in the same place all the time. The satellite retransmits your call 22,335 miles down again, where a similar "dish" antenna in Europe receives it and routes it to its destination.

Telephone company central offices are present-day models for science fiction environments. Security is very tight, with all sorts of color-coded badges and heavy, locked doors. In many central offices, an operating company shares a building with one or more long distance carriers, so employees of either company often do not have access to the other's space. Within, you see the big switches themselves, long rows of electronic components arrayed like aisles in a supermarket. Overhead are the cable racks where thick gray cables, each containing hundreds of color-coded wires, run hither and yon between the fluorescent-lit equipment rows.

The system is carefully designed to save precious seconds on every call. As soon as the area code is dialed, the system begins looking for an available path to that location while storing the remaining digits as they are dialed. As soon as the long distance path comes up, the system sends the three "exchange" digits over it to look for the destination exchange while still holding the last four. When the path opens to the destination exchange, the last four digits go across it to find that one telephone the customer wants to reach.

For many years, Western Electric manufactured mechanical "crossbar" switches for telephone company central offices, with Rolls Royce quality; each switch was designed to last forty years in everyday service. Even today in the old rural telephone buildings, the "snap, snap, snap" of the mechanical relays is relentless. More recent switches are electronic; tones and voices race along wires and through microchips in absolute silence. Ironically, these electronic switching systems are potentially even more durable, but early versions were not modular. Like the ancient pictographs, they could not be readily adapted to new requirements. The early electronic switches were usually considered obsolete and replaced after only a decade.

The newest electronic switches are controlled primarily by software and are completely modular in design. When a new feature is needed, it can be programmed in, and when more capacity is needed, additional "line cards" can be installed. These switches can handle voice and data simultaneously, and they should remain in place for the foreseeable future.

All this replacement and change is driven by competition. In today's deregulated environment, large corporations can literally set up their own systems and completely bypass the telephone operating companies. The local telephone operating companies are thus scrambling to compete with private telecommunications equipment companies.

When telephone engineers design a network, they estimate how much traffic it will carry and plan for the required "grade of service." Grade of service is the percentage of calls initiated that do not go through because all circuits in that direction are busy; 1 percent is considered excellent, 5 percent is tolerable.

Traffic volume varies from hour to hour. Telephone engineers measure grade of service during the busiest hour of an average day, so service is actually much better during off-peak hours. Of course, the system then is overloaded on peak days such as Mothers' Day or Christmas; on those days, callers will get a lot of busy signals. Systems are sized thus to keep costs down; every circuit costs money to install and maintain. The system could easily be designed so that, even on peak calling days, every call gets through on the first try, but the cost, inevitably passed on to the public, would be exorbitant.

Even so, having a system in which circuits are usually ready and waiting means that some sit idle most of the time. But nowhere do John Milton's words ring more true: "They also serve who only stand and wait." You can usually distinguish a "circuit busy," or an overall telephone network overload, from a "line busy," where the telephone being called is in use, by the type of busy signal. Short, fast beeps indicate a circuit busy, while slower beeps indicate a line busy. But not always. Some telephone operating companies hide a poor grade of service by using the slower line busy signal for both situations. If you call someone and encounter an unexpected "line busy," try again and ask whether the line had just been in use.

The overall service quality of a telephone system is based primarily on its grade of service and its audio quality. Good audio is clear with a quiet background. It also costs the telephone company more than mediocre audio; as usual, you get what you pay for.

MA BELL AND HER KIDS

The United States has the only major free enterprise telephone system in the world, although other countries are exploring the idea. One day we will reflect with Robert Frost:

> Two roads diverged in a wood, and I—
> I took the one less traveled by,
> And that has made all the difference.

Why the Kids Left Home

Once upon a time, telephones were only in wealthy

homes. Many working-class people in the cities could not afford the actual cost of installation, and rural areas were extremely expensive to wire; a farmhouse a mile from its neighbor needed a mile of wire just for itself.

The federal government looked forward to the day when every American home would have a telephone, and it encouraged AT & T to pursue "universal service." AT & T set long distance rates above cost and used the profit to subsidize local service.

AT & T was "the telephone company." It offered quality equipment at low prices but firmly insisted that only its own phones be connected to the network. It had a commitment to reliability and felt that it could be responsible only if it had total control over what was connected to its network.

This conservative approach set a higher priority on reliability than on innovation; Bell System equipment was invariably "tried and true." But the Age of Aquarius came, and America was feeling innovative. In 1968 a suit by Carterfone Communications Corporation against AT & T ended with a ruling that AT & T must allow customers to connect non-Bell equipment to its network.

In 1974 the United States Department of Justice filed an antitrust suit against AT & T. The suit alleged that AT & T's ownership of nearly the entire telephone system eliminated the possibility of competition. It did not matter that the Bell System had provided the world's best telephone service for a century. AT & T attorneys and United States Government attorneys brought carton after carton of documents to the court of Judge Harold H. Greene.

While Judge Greene pored over legal documents, outside his courtroom the telecommunications industry was changing dramatically. It became more and more difficult to say exactly what was telephone equipment and what wasn't. A private branch exchange, or PBX, is a computer on the user's premises dedicated to the task of telephone line switching; is it telephone equipment or a computer? Suppose it also stores telephone numbers and telephone messages and performs phone system usage and cost analyses as programmed by the user? Does it matter that the telephone company's central office systems also complete usage analyses and compute bills?

A telephone instrument is an electronic interface between a person and a phone line. A microcomputer with a built-in modem is also an electronic interface between a person and a phone line, although it isn't a voice transducer and it does not look like a telephone. These microcomputers were wired together into switched networks by contractors who weren't telephone company people, but the networks worked pretty much the same way AT & T's did. More important, the advent of microwave stations and satellites meant that independent common carriers could move information without using buried wires. Distinctions between telephone equipment, radio equipment, and computer equipment would forever run behind the pace of innovation.

The genie was out of the bottle, and there was no coaxing it back. Judge Greene felt it was inadvisable to let old AT & T, a regulated monopoly, compete in the open computer market because it would be too easy to charge more for phone service and use the extra profit to sell computers for less than the competition could. As corporate communications equipment and data-processing equipment merged into data management systems, the demarcation began to look even more arbitrary and capricious.

At the same time, the independent common carriers began to provide long distance service at less cost than old AT & T. The independents didn't have to subsidize local service. They competed for the more profitable long distance calls from one major city to another, while leaving AT & T the less profitable small-town long distance service, which it was forced to continue. Some of the other common carriers used lower-cost, lower-quality long distance circuits, leaving AT & T responsible for providing top quality service. Something had to give. You can't tell one competitor that it can operate as freely as the wind and another that it must pay heavy subsidies and take the work no one else wants.

In countries where the national government owns all the big communications common carriers—the telephone network as well as the post office—this problem does not arise; the government simply provides end-to-end connections and lets private industry plug in compatible computers. There are no stockholders or competition.

At first there were proposals that the Bell System remain intact but abandon "universal service" and make each section of the business pay its own way. But that doesn't work in a tightly integrated business any more than it does in a close-knit family. Company managers would inevitably try to subsidize local business lines and long distance service at the expense of captive residential customers. It would take an army of government regulators to prevent such subsidies, and the telephone companies would hire their own army of accounting technicians to meet the challenge. Rather than expend all this customer revenue and tax money, divestiture assures that each line of business pays for its own costs.

AT & T, from its perspective of decades, anticipated that its local operating companies would probably always be rate regulated by state public utility commissions. It also saw that the information management industry, with its mainframes, PBX's, and microcomputers, was free of price regulation and earned higher average rates of return on investment. Its management reasoned that, as long as it had the local telephone operating monopoly, it could never be an information management company.

Old AT & T was the most powerful corporation in the world. It could have kept a thousand lawyers working for a thousand years on the antitrust case. Old AT & T also had enough political clout to do well in Congress. But instead, it quietly agreed to its own dismemberment.

Telecommunications engineers had generally favored keeping the Bell System intact. Bell had built the world's most advanced and reliable telephone network. More important, from the chairman of the board on down, old AT & T had a "service ethic," a belief that customer satisfaction was the most important thing in the world. Everything was internally coordinated; customers could have the systems they wanted with one-stop shopping.

Business managers, however, felt that divestiture was the only way to introduce a whirlwind of communications technology and release some of Bell's advanced computer systems through competition. By 1982 the managers had won. On January 1, 1984, lightning struck and the Bell System, with its service ethic, was shattered.

How to Tell the Kids Apart

A company that makes extensive use of satellites will find its cost for a three thousand-mile call the same as for a three hundred-mile call and can charge a nearly flat rate, modified only to meet competition. A company using a land-based network will tie more of it up on a longer distance call and charge accordingly. One company might have a lot of business customers who only use their phones during the day, so it offers steep night discounts for otherwise unused traffic capacity; another company, with mostly residential customers, will have a more even distribution of calls and therefore charge less for day calls and more for evening ones. The canny customer looks at all the rate structures and then finds the one best fitted to his or her own calling pattern.

Many customers use two or more services; if a customer finds that one carrier charges less for calls to her brother in Pennsylvania while another charges less for calls to her sister in Maryland, she uses each to best advantage. Also, when she calls her mother in Florida on Mother's Day and all the circuits are busy, she tries another carrier to see if it can get through! Big business does it all the time with "automatic route selection."

This is easily done. Every long distance carrier connected to your local telephone company has a special "dialing prefix." If you dial long distance using only the prefix "1," the call will go out to the long distance company you selected—and which you can change at any time. Say your chosen carrier is MCI, you can dial a number like "10288" instead of "1" to place the call over AT & T facilities. Check with your local telephone company to find out which long distance companies are available in your area, what their prefixes are, and whether there is a surcharge for using a carrier other than your chosen one.

For corporations, divestiture has brought a tidal wave of new system options and savings. For the public, results are mixed so far. Monthly charges for basic service have gone way up. Long distance charges are way down. It costs less in the long run to own a phone than to lease one, so people with several phones in the house save money. Divestiture helped the upper middle class both by opening up more timesaving innovations and by saving money overall. It increased costs for a working class less apt to use timesaving innovations, to make long distance calls, or to own several phones.

The Kids Are Independent

The best force for setting standards is a single, dominant company. When AT & T owned the Bell operating companies, its standards were absolute. When the giant made its decisions, other players followed, because it was in their interest to be compatible.

The government is second best. Its decisions tend to be political; each company, knowing what new projects are in its own research labs, lobbies Congress and the Federal Communications Commission to go in that direction. The divergent pulling and tugging can produce some anomalies, such as the FCC's AM stereo "decision" in which it was unable to select and so authorized four incompatible systems simultaneously. Also, when standards have the force of law, progress can be inhibited.

Standards agreed upon by committees are enforced simply through companies' fears of being odd man out; they work very well in most situations when it really doesn't matter what the standard is as long as everyone agrees on it. They are no match, however, for a company that believes it can dominate the market with a new product.

Communication depends on consistency, on a nationwide system of shared protocols constantly updated. In that respect, if in no other, we will miss Ma Bell.

When Polish General Wojciech Jaruszelski declared martial law in December 1981, the first thing he did was turn off Poland's entire telephone system. Solidarity protesters had no opportunity to organize a response, and Lech Walesa's union was broken. General Jaruszelski knew that information exchange is an integral part of political freedom. Control and limit the information available to people and you can control and limit their beliefs, decisions, and actions.

In the United States, sources of information have been

decentralized since the early history of the republic. We have more TV stations, newspapers, magazines, and public information utilities than any other people who have ever lived on Earth. Personal computers that we can use to analyze all this information are widely distributed in our population.

Divestiture added decentralized movement of private information from one place to another. There are large telephone companies and small telephone companies of every kind. It might once have been possible for an American political institution to order Ma Bell to shut down, but not now. In place of Ma Bell, we have seven regional telephone operating companies, all sorts of long distance common carriers, and thousands of corporations that would have to be reached and convinced by the Federal Emergency Management Agency.

The federal program to control telephone use in a national emergency is called "line load control." Coordinated through the local tariffed telephone companies, it restricts dial tone primarily to senior officials while allowing any telephone to receive incoming calls. The telephone companies would impose it to assure that key officials could get through to one another in an emergency, but not to support a crackdown on American civil liberties.

Divestiture would pose a formidable challenge in a time of national emergency; the Pentagon made a strong effort to stop divestiture based on genuine concern about mobilizing a decentralized system.

The Dilemma of Freedom

Universal service was a good idea, but implementing it was so expensive that old Ma Bell took profits from everywhere else to subsidize it—long distance revenues, yellow pages sales, and business service. The loss of revenue from business service, in particular, has been a major problem since divestiture.

Before divestiture, business telephone service had massively subsidized residential service, but businesses can now bypass local telephone operating companies by using independent PBX's. The telcos have to meet the competition by providing business service at the same price as the independents, that is, for cost plus a small profit margin. There is then no money left to subsidize residential service.

Residential customers are becoming alarmed as charges rise to meet costs. Since residential customers vote, state regulators try to force charges down, reducing local telephone company profit margins. As a result, the telcos, now more independent, are trying harder to diversify into more profitable lines of business such as long distance and even international calling, manufacturing equipment, and providing information services such as electronic "yellow pages," shopping and making bank transactions from home, handling airline reservations, and distributing news and editorials. Residential service has sometimes been treated as a sideline.

Our unique national telecommunications system has rate regulated companies competing with unregulated companies for the same large commercial accounts.

Constant problems and ever more complicated "solutions" will continue unless the regulators support the same pricing principle as the competitive, free enterprise side uses—prices reflect costs, without exception.

So far, state regulators have not supported this pricing system. Flat rate call pricing is available in most states. For instance, a telemarketer working out of a home with a flat rate telephone line can make two hundred local calls a day for the same price as a subscriber who makes two local calls a day. Since revenues have to cover costs, the two-call customer is subsidizing the telemarketer.

Part of the solution is Local Measured Service. LMS is a billing arrangement in which local calls are billed by time and distance. Properly implemented, it charges a very low basic monthly rate. Most of the cost is based on time and distance, exactly as long distance calls are billed now. The cost for an average user, including usage, should be less than the cost for a flat rate line. Charging for local calls results in lower usage of the system, so the companies' expansion costs will be down. "Call detail recording" equipment costs a lot less than most local telephone operating companies will save.

LMS should be mandatory for all subscribers, business and residential. In most states, business lobbies have neutered LMS by making it optional so that heavy users still get the flat rate free ride.

LMS will not force local telephone operating companies to be outgunned in the competition for corporations. If prices accurately reflect costs, then companies offering "bypass" services will compete on a level playing field and hold down costs for all.

From the beginning, businesses have used telephone service more than residential customers. As a result, Ma Bell, faced with heavy use of its circuits during regular business hours as compared with evenings and weekends, sold spare long distance service at steep discounts. We have all become accustomed to this little bonus.

Long distance carriers compete only with one another for residential and small business service. Competing with megacorporate private networks is tougher, since a private network is tailored to specific requirements. The common carriers, under pressure to come in with the lowest possible prices for business service, have reduced daytime costs and increased evening and weekend costs to compete for the big accounts.

Long distance competition will produce some benefit for residential long distance users, however. In the effort to compete with private networks, the carriers will add new features. Once installed, most will be available for use by all subscribers.

Divestiture put the telcos squarely into an identity crisis. For decades they had thought of themselves as public utilities, staid old maiden aunts. Now they are Silicon Valley gunslingers. Ameritech, Bell Atlantic, Bell South, Nynex, Pacific Telesis, Southwestern Bell, and U.S. West are separate companies now. Each will do as well as its market and political strengths allow.

TODAY'S TECHNOLOGY

The lively and diverse telecommunications industry has already put systems in place that will lead us into the brave new world to come.

Cellular Radio Telephones

Until a few years ago, car telephones had a special problem. To cover a major metropolitan area, each channel had to serve the entire area. Otherwise, you could be cruising along the street enjoying your phone conversation when you suddenly got out of range. But a citywide repeater could only support one conversation on each channel. There were only a few channels available in each area, so the citywide system could support only a few users at a time.

The cellular mobile network solves that problem. It consists of a lot of low-powered repeaters scattered around a metropolitan area, all connected by leased telephone lines to a central control point. When a subscriber wants to make a call from her car, she enters the desired phone number into the mobile telephone and presses a button to start the process. The phone transmits the calling and destination phone numbers. They are picked up by several of the low-powered repeaters and carried back to the control computer. The control computer selects the repeater that best received the call and uses it to connect the subscriber.

As the subscriber continues to drive, she gradually leaves the coverage area, or "cell," of the original repeater and enters the coverage area of another. The control computer continues to monitor her transmissions; as soon as the signal into the new repeater is stronger than that into the original, the control computer begins to transmit back to the subscriber through the new one. As she continues to drive from one cell to the next, the control computer continues to "follow" her. The subscriber knows only that her phone call is clear and strong everywhere in the metropolitan area.

The system is even smarter than that, however. If the driver passes into a cell where a conversation is already in progress, the control computer silently looks for a vacant channel and begins transmitting on it. At the same time, it directs the mobile phone to transmit and receive on the new channel! It can also tell the mobile phone to increase power as it gets near the edge of its range or decrease as it gets close to the repeater so that nearby conversations are not disturbed.

When the cellular companies were seeking government approval, they explained that, as the number of subscribers increases, they would accommodate the additional calling volume by increasing the number of low powered repeaters so that each one covered a smaller area. Now that they are established, the industry is politically trying to flank the FCC by pressing for more channels per repeater, instead. More channels for cellular service means they are expanding at the expense of whoever had those channels before. There's old John Donne again; no communications service is an island.

Service will be expanded to meet the need, however. Cellular technology means that everyone who wants one can have a mobile telephone. But one way or another, a good grade of service costs more. Before you select a cellular carrier, find out what grade of service is guaranteed.

Fiber Optic Cable

Modern long distance telephone cables are no longer made of copper. The new cables are long, thin strands of glass designed to carry light beams over remarkable distances. They pass data faster than satellites do, without a time lag. They have enough bandwidth to handle all the communications we could ever want without overcrowding.

In cross section, a fiber optic cable looks like a donut. The slim, glass, center core, usually fifty microns in diameter, is entirely surrounded by glass cladding with a lower index of refraction, which in turn is surrounded by a protective polymer jacket. The light has to come straight in so that it just grazes the core; entry at even a slight angle will cause it to bounce around and quickly dissipate. Since, inevitably, the light refracts and reflects off the surface of the core, losing power as it does, regenerative repeaters are installed at strategic locations.

The light itself comes from injection laser diodes or light-emitting diodes. An injection laser diode pulsing a trillion times per second gives enough bandwidth to carry millions of voice conversations, once we develop the technology and the need to encode that many; it also lasts an average one million hours before needing replacement. The more familiar light-emitting diode offers considerably less bandwidth and only one-tenth the projected service life at less than half the price. It is safer in use, and so can be operated by workers with less expertise. Although it's called fiber "optic" cable, the light is deep infrared, far below the visible spectrum.

The Department of Defense promotes fiber optic cable in long range communications wherever possible. It radiates no magnetic field as copper wire does, nor does it travel over open country as microwaves do. It is extremely difficult to monitor a fiber optic conversation outside a telephone company central office, since it can only be done by inserting a special receiver through the outer cladding at the very edge of the waveguide. Fiber optic cables are also immune to electrical storm interference and to electromagnetic pulse radiation in the event of a nuclear blast.

The Sky's the Limit

Look up! Beyond the rooftops, far above the New York World Trade Center and the Sears Tower, far above the highest aerie, far above Mount Everest, far above where the highest jet aircraft fly, far above the van Allen radiation belts, nearly one-tenth of the way to the moon, is a Saturnlike ring of man-made objects.

The sky is crowded up there. All in a row, at exactly the same 22,335-mile altitude, they lazily circle the distant, blue-and-white planet below once every twenty-four hours. These communications satellites, put up over the western hemisphere by such giants as AT & T, Comsat General, Hughes, RCA, and the governments of Canada and Mexico, are often no more than a thousand miles apart. This distance seems far enough for a satellite small enough to fit in your living room except for its solar power collector "wings," but if you could look up and see them the way an "earth station" does, they would appear only a few degrees apart and in the same frequency range.

A geosynchronous communications satellite is really just a radio repeater in the sky. But when the curvature of the Earth is the obstacle we want to go above, only a satellite is high enough to do the job.

An earth station is a base station. It consists of a parabolic or "dish" antenna aimed directly at a satellite, a microwave transmitter and receiver, and some telephone interconnect and control equipment. A teleport is the same thing, only much bigger and operating as a host for smaller satellite communications systems operated by many companies.

A dish antenna works like a camera buff's telescopic mirror lens. In both cases, the idea is to concentrate narrowly on something very far away. When receiving, it is designed to reflect microwave signals from a very precise direction hitting any part of the dish to a very small reflector mounted above the center of the dish. The reflector in turn bounces the signals even more narrowly toward a small microwave receiving antenna mounted in the center of the dish. These antennas are extremely directional; signals hitting the big dish from even a slightly different angle will be reflected to a point near the small reflector but not onto it and will never be focused on the small receiving antenna itself.

The transmitting dish antenna does the same thing in reverse; a signal is put out by the transmitting antenna and aimed directly at the small reflector, which bounces it accurately onto the whole surface of the main dish, which in turn reflects the signal like a continuous stream of parallel arrows directly at the satellite.

Satellites are a magnificent achievement. They allow big companies to completely bypass the telephone companies, which in turn forces the telephone companies to offer more service at less cost. They enable rural areas, especially in rugged terrain, to have complete telecommunications systems, which means all kinds of economic development in places that never had wire line systems. But they are not pie in the sky.

One problem with satellite communication is the time it takes to get a signal up to the satellite and down again. Radio signals travel at about 186,000 miles per second. The round trip up to the satellite and back is about 45,000 miles, so it takes about one-quarter of a second to get a signal from the transmitting station to the receiving station. Since in most communications the signal is intended to elicit a response that must also make the round trip, the total delay between question and answer is about half a second.

In a telephone conversation, the lag means a brief pause as each person waits for the other's response, but these days we tolerate it for the benefit of reliable overseas telephone calls.

THE BRAVE NEW WORLD

The integrated services digital network, called "ISDN," is coming. It will be the most dramatic change in telecommunications since crank telephones were replaced by dial phones half a century ago.

Your telephone today generates an electrical analog of your voice to send over the wire. It is a literal analog: When your voice is loud, there is more voltage; between syllables and words, the voltage drops. The problem with analog is its limited information-carrying capacity. An end-to-end analog call can carry just one voice per channel. If you want your personal computer to talk with another computer by phone, you have to put the signal through a modem to get analog signals the line can send. This process slows the information transfer rate way down. The receiving user then needs a modem to convert the signal back into digital form.

When digital telephone lines arrive, we will have to replace all our telephones with new digital phones. Each digital phone will have a "codec," or "*co*der-*dec*oder," in it to convert our analog voices into a stream of ones and zeros. Codecs are common in telephone systems today. They are used as gateways to telephone company digital switch networks. The integrated services digital network, like all networks, is being built one switch at a time.

All that underground copper wire and fiber optic cable are very expensive. Since a lot of digital streams can be packed together on a single telephone line, each line will do a lot more work for the same cost. Also, digital equipment is a lot smaller and more compact than its analog counterparts. If you took all the telephone company central offices today and put them together, you'd have a city the size of St. Louis. All that plant and equipment costs a bundle, too. If the telcos can save money, consumers will be able to recover some of it.

Audio quality will be perfect with the all-digital system; even overseas phone calls will have "in the next room" clarity. There will be no background noise; between syllables or words, the line will be silent.

All transmission lines add noise and attenuate signal, so they need repeaters every so often. The old analog repeaters had to amplify the noise along with voice signals. The new digital regenerative repeaters generate a brand new identical signal, without accumulated noise, and send it on to the next regenerative repeater. Digital telephones will have better microphones and speakers to take advantage of the crystal clear audio.

Also, digital audio is just a stream of ones and zeros. The system has to contend with only two states, so the waveforms are extremely simple. By comparison, the complex waveforms of the human voice are far more demanding; compare, for instance, the French *des cieux* and *des yeux.*

These digital voice streams will run at about 64,000 bits (ones and zeros) per second. So the line to your house will be capable of carrying 64,000 bits per second for voice use.

Today's standard voice digitizing system, called pulse

code modulation, samples the human voice 8,000 times per second. Each sample is converted into an eight-bit code, for a total of 64,000 bits per second. But engineers know that information in human speech is not spread evenly over time; some parts of the speech waveform carry more information than others. Consequently, researchers are studying how acoustic energy is converted into the electrical signals that are sent over aural nerves to the brain; if some parts are lost during conversion anyway, they reason, why transmit them? A new technique, called multipulse linear predictive coding, promises to reduce that 64,000 bits per second all the way down to 2,400 bits per second as soon as processors fast enough to eliminate the excess information can be mass produced at reasonable cost. We could then have several telephone conversations at once on a single line. At 2,400 bits per second, even with several conversations at once, there would still be plenty of room left on a 64,000 bit-per-second line. Families with teenagers will appreciate that. The telephone operating companies could use the remaining bandwidth to provide us all with additional services or lower prices.

In addition to all that, a separate data access, also capable of moving 64,000 bits per second, is coming. If you commit the entire capacity to one use, it could move about two single-spaced, typed pages of text every second. Of course, you could also subdivide it and run several other systems at the same time.

Every house today has a data terminal: the mailbox. In the next decade, it will be more economical to use a modern data terminal, one with a video display and keyboard, so most of us will buy one. It will handle the transactions now handled by mail more efficiently; we will get news and feature stories, arrange airline and hotel reservations, pay bills, shop, and, in some cases, earn a good living through our data terminals, all while the kids do school research projects on their terminals. Some of the 64,000 bits per second will go for encryption; our banks will give each of us a personal identification number that our terminals will use to decode incoming financial information and encode outgoing information so it cannot be read by unauthorized persons. The new data terminals will also accommodate purposes the old one never did. Hospitals will track outpatient status through electronic measuring devices that now serve intensive care units. Energy and water utilities will be able to check usage by phone—on the same telephone line, at the same time as conversation.

There will also be another data access, a "low speed" one, that will carry "only" 16,000 bits per second. It will be used for "call setup." In addition to the "touch-tones" there are various signals, most of them inaudible, that travel over your telephone line. One kind signals the phone company that you've lifted the receiver and want a dial tone, another, that the other party has picked up the phone and the system can start timing the call for billing, and so forth. The digital phones of the next decade will have much more setup signaling to match their new capabilities.

This format, one high-speed voice channel, one high-speed data channel, and one low-speed setup channel, seems like more than anyone will ever use.

When a subdivision is built a long way from town,

they build a road. At first it is practically empty and everyone says, look at the expensive road they built way out in the sticks. After a while another subdivision is built, then a third, then a fourth, then many. The traffic builds up until everyone who commutes on that road says they should have planned ahead and put in more lanes.

Planning for more lanes is already underway! Farther down the road is a "wideband ISDN," carrying a phenomenal 1,544,000 bits per second over a single phone line. At that rate, we can get high-definition picture phone service along with everything else. We will use this communicating power for data, too. The sum of human knowledge is still doubling every ten years. We will need better ways of moving it to where it's needed.

When comes the revolution, we won't call them phones. They'll be called "voice terminals," a counterpart term for "data terminals." We'll be so far from "plain old telephone service" that the word *"telephone"* will be too imprecise for practical use and will gradually disappear into the twenty-first century.

Chapter 6

BUSINESS SYSTEMS

The global economy is upon us. American homes have Japanese television sets in the family room, English bone china in the dining room, Swiss chocolates in the living room, Italian shoes in the closet, and a German car in the garage. This international environment is even more evident in business; individual components for a single product can be manufactured in a dozen countries and the product itself sold in a dozen others. Despite the recent protectionist movement, we are all multinationals now.

Information has become the racer's edge. The company that knows more about the manufacture and transportation of its outsourced components can build its products more efficiently. The company that knows more about the current sales trends on six continents can sell more efficiently. Efficiency means survival. Managers and employees who can move information from one mind to another more efficiently will have the racer's edge.

PRIVATE TELEPHONE NETWORKS

In the old days, when the Bell System was "the telephone company," there was one main network. Now, telephone networks sprout like plants in a rain forest.

Small Networks

The most basic telephone networks are installed in small organizations. Say an organization has a hundred employees who need telephones on their desks. If each of these employees is on the phone most of the day, everyone will need a line. If, however, each is actually on the phone only a few minutes a day, those one hundred lines would sit idle most of the time.

A less expensive alternative would be for the company to rent ten special lines called "access lines" from the local telephone operating company and to install a small PBX on its own premises. This system would allow all one hundred employees to use the ten access lines on a shared basis. It works exactly like a telephone company central office, only it is much smaller and privately owned. The local telco reserves a block of ten access lines and one hundred numbers. When someone from the outside calls one of the numbers, the telco routes the call to the organization over any of the ten access lines. The PBX "recognizes" the number and routes the call to the right desk. Similarly, when an employee picks up the phone, the PBX connects it to an available access line and the call goes out as usual.

Bypass

Lily Tomlin used to do a comic skit as a telephone operator named Ernestine who always described the telephone company as "omnipotent." Today's telephone companies are not at all omnipotent. PBXs can directly access the intermachine trunk lines to a long distance carrier's network, entirely bypassing the local telephone company.

Building managers are competing with the telcos these days by offering "shared tenant" service. Large office buildings already provide heat, light, air conditioning, and other onsite services; why not telephone service? The managers buy a single big digital PBX with special partitioning circuitry and sell its advanced features and services to all the tenants at less than what the telcos charge.

The Fortune 500 companies have gone in a lot deeper. Nearly all these companies have PBXs and so can bypass the local telephone companies. Most have tie lines and private long distance networks so that at least intracompany calls go out over their own facilities. Quite a few have invested in long distance transmission facilities including microwave, satellites, fiber optic lines, and two-way cable television; they literally have private end-to-end telephone companies. The Bell telephone companies and public long distance carriers hardly participate at all in this type of bypass. And since many Fortune 500 companies are no longer telephone company customers, the revenue that no longer flows into telephone companies has to be replaced by increasing the cost to residential and small business users.

To keep large users as customers, the Bell telephone operating companies are setting up and operating bypass systems of their own. Although they are literally bypassing themselves, they can offer fixed prices over specified periods of time as well as economies of scale and expertise.

DIGITAL COMMUNICATION

Digital communication moves information in machine readable form from one place to another. It works the same way human communication does.

When one person calls another, the person called begins the interaction by saying "hello." The caller then identifies and checks, by voice recognition or direct question, the identity of the person who picked up the phone. Each caller then semiconsciously ascertains the other's condition to decide whether a relaxed or rapid-fire pace is appropriate. The information exchange then starts. When the information exchange is complete, one party initiates a closing protocol, perhaps by summarizing the contents of the conversation, and both parties sign off.

There are other specific protocols. If the calling party says, "Is Mr. Smith there," and Mr. Smith is the one who answered the phone, Mr. Smith says, "Speaking!" This might be followed by the pecking order protocol, "Mr. Smith, please hold for Mr. Jones."

Of course, computers communicate entirely in ones and zeros. Computers send the letter "e," for instance, as "01100101." When computers are connected directly to one another the "1" is represented by a few volts, while the "0" is represented by no voltage. So "e" is represented by off-on-on-off-off-on-off-on.

But, in their own way, the computers are doing what humans do. They should; after all, we program them! The computer initiating the contact signals its presence and the other responds. They briefly and silently "handshake," or exchange information needed to understand one another. They then say what their human masters want them to say, and hang up.

ELECTRONIC MESSAGES

Electronic message systems are used when two or more executives are rarely available for communication simultaneously. Each can communicate when a moment is available.

Electronic Mail

Electronic mail, or E-mail, usually carries short, time-sensitive messages. Character format is best for messages that have facts and figures but little emotional content.

The originator sits down at an E-mail work station and composes a message. The message can be revised on screen. When the sender is ready, the message can be transmitted either to one recipient or simultaneously to many. At a convenient time, each recipient enters the system and notes, perhaps, that several messages are waiting. The messages are listed by originator, date, and often, subject. The recipient indicates an interest in reading some or all, and the system scrolls the desired messages through. The recipient can often reply on the spot, and the replies become available on each originator's computer within moments.

E-mail moves text efficiently. As in most forms of communication, E-mail content and metamessage convey separate kinds of information. The content is *what* the message says; the metamessage is *how* the message says it.

An E-Mail message starts with the "Subject" header. A precise description motivates the recipient to read the message, suggests that the sender is competent, and makes it easy to retrieve the message from the archive six months later.

Creating and perfecting are different mental processes; both cannot be done at the same time. A message often has to be revised more than once before it is literate, and it should be clear, concise, and precise. Proper punctuation counts; even James Joyce didn't use stream-of-consciousness for his business letters. Upper and lower case add a graceful patina; if all lower case didn't help e.e. cummings, it won't help anyone. Since most E-mail systems don't edit text, users whose metamessage is "professional quality" generally prepare their messages off-line on a word processor first.

Humor is usually signaled by voice inflections and body signals. Since E-mail is straight text, the smiley face :-) is used instead to signal humor. Look at it sideways.

Voice Mail

About one business caller in four reaches the desired party on the first try. The other three leave a message. Answering machines automate the game of telephone tag. They handle very short messages in simple situations well.

Voice mail bypasses telephone tag. It is used when there is very little time to compose a message, when one person needs to address many, and when users travel. Modern voice mail systems digitize the human voice, or convert it into a stream of zeros and ones. In that form, the voice signal can be distributed very efficiently.

In-house systems use voice mail to replace the ubiquitous interoffice memo. Voice mail takes less time to originate and send. Executives can use group codes to reach many employees with a single message, and the systems can even indicate who didn't get the message. The voice mail systems automatically dial the addressee's telephone number and make a digitized announcement that this is a voice mail call. A computer-generated voice then asks the person who picked up the phone to key in a private access code. Once the system is satisfied that an authorized addressee is on the line, the computer voice "reads" the message.

Voice mail systems usually ask a second time if the access code is not given, or given incorrectly. After two or three tries, however, most will hang up and try again later. They will also hang up and try later if the phone is busy or not answered within a programmed number of seconds.

Local voice messages are sent immediately. Routine long distance and overseas messages are sometimes held until telephone rates are lowest and then sent in batches. Both kinds are often kept on file for up to thirty days, even after they have been received, for easy reference.

Far-flung sales representatives can usually call the headquarters voice mail system via an "800" telephone number. Representatives can leave messages to production and distribution contacts, receive messages from all over the company as well as from customers, and reply on the spot.

Brevity is absolutely necessary with voice mail; most recipients have a short concentration span. Since creating and perfecting are different mental processes for voice mail too, many users will convey a more positive image by writing out the message ahead of time and reading it into the system. It takes a little longer, but then quality always does.

Message Priorities

Senders and receivers have opposing interests. Senders usually want unrestricted access. Recipients, especially senior managers, are too busy to respond to everyone in the organization, so they want selective access.

Access systems controlled by senders have a priority system, and the sender can indicate the level of importance—"routine," "urgent," etc. But some senders think everything they send is urgent. Guidelines can help managers restrict the use of priority designators to critical messages, but only if managers retrieve their messages reasonably often will senders feel confident designating messages "routine."

Access systems controlled by recipients are based on the sender's identity. Typically, all senders in a business hierarchy above the recipient, specified senders at the recipient's own level, and senders supervised directly by the recipient are authorized. This system usually works pretty well, but the content ultimately determines the importance of a message; sometimes important messages come from unexpected senders.

Some message systems do not allow senders to change a message before the recipient gets it. Dynamic institutions move fast; sometimes a message can be overtaken by events within hours. If new information obsoletes a message, the sender should be able to change or delete it at any time before the recipient gets it.

FACSIMILE

Facsimile transmits images. It is used for documents containing designs, patterns, graphs, charts, and signatures.

It works by scanning an entire page from top to bottom and then converting every tiny dot into telephone compatible signals. Another "fax" machine at the receiving location reads these signals, putting a dot everywhere one is indicated. The image formed by these dots is the same as on the original.

It takes more dots to copy the image of a page than to send a page of straight text, so facsimile transmission might take longer. But when images are needed, facsimile is very useful.

LOCAL AREA NETWORKS

A local area network, or LAN, is a group of terminals or computers wired so that all access a central file server, printer, modem, and other resources.

There are different kinds of LANs. Sometimes one very powerful minicomputer with all its resources is used by many dumb terminals. Dumb terminals have keyboards and screens, as personal computers do, but instead of microprocessors and disk drives they have only built-in modems, like an office with one boss and a group of clericals. In many modern systems, each user has a fully equipped microcomputer; a central system assigns background processing tasks to each such computer. "Distributed processing" configurations can be very efficient.

Small LANs, and older LANs, are hard-wired together. For example, a "star" configuration sets up the main resources at the center and runs cable to each work station. State of the art LANs, especially larger ones, are connected via telephone lines through a digital switch network for more flexible system size, message routing, and office reorganization.

Either way, the idea is that work stations share information or resources. Imagine a big mail order house with twenty people receiving telephone orders for products. Since all the work stations have access to the same inventory database, if a product is sold out or re-priced, all stations asking for that product will immediately know.

The other important function of local area networks is moving data or text from one work station to another. A staffer can draft a memo on his own terminal, then type in a code to send it to his supervisor's terminal. The supervisor might make some changes, then type a code so that the document appears on the manager's terminal. The manager approves it and routes it for transmission to the recipient. If the recipient is part of the same work group, the message will be sent over the local area network. Mail for more distant recipients can be routed over an electronic mail system; no LAN is an island.

Synergy is the mark of an excellent LAN. For instance, some allow the user to write letters whose specifics are directly linked to a database. If a price change or mailing address change is entered into the database, all letters linked to it are automatically updated as well. These LANs invariably contain a lot of "human engineering," accommodating to the way humans resolve day to day situations.

TELECONFERENCING

A teleconference is a phone call with three or more participants. Today, the practical limit on participation is imposed by human factors; the more active participants in a meeting, the more discipline and control it takes to keep it an organized vehicle of communication. A fairly large teleconference is like a fairly large meeting. A moderator maintains a list of participants, announces each agenda item, calls on first one participant and then another for comments or questions, and summarizes conclusions and decisions.

A well-run teleconference usually has an attendant, an employee with three basic responsibilities. First, the attendant uses a list of approved participants and announces newcomers. People dialing into the teleconference have to be screened; no competitors are invited! Second, although today's best conference bridges can bring together fifty or more people, human operators still have to adjust the equipment on occasion so each participant's voice sounds clear and natural. Third, the attendant keeps a record of the conference. Some companies ask their attendants to record the teleconference and provide a cassette to anyone who requests one; participants, of course, should be aware that such recordings are routinely made. Others ask the attendant to keep a written record of major points and commitments.

Program managers can set up regularly scheduled teleconferences with their regional managers. Suppose a teleconference is set up for every Monday morning at eight o'clock Pacific time. On the first Monday of every month, district managers, as well as regional managers, are brought in on a bigger teleconference so that all can feel part of the team. The headquarters manager sets an agenda, often based on suggestions by the regional managers. On each topic, policy is clarified, ideas are exchanged, and action schedules are established. Participants make notes ahead of time on what they want to say so that when their turn comes, they are efficient and well organized. They also take notes during the teleconference on what has been said or agreed to.

Regular teleconferences enable program managers all over the country to work with their counterparts as a team. Each participant gets the big picture, and the same picture. Higher management then has more confidence in the program as a whole.

PUBLIC DATA NETWORKS

When you mail a letter, you put it in a packet or envelope. You add an address. You put the letter into a mailbox with a lot of other letters. The letters are carried to a post office where a sorter reads the address and puts it in the proper bin. The mail in that bin is taken to another post office much nearer the recipient, where another sorter reads the address and puts the letter in another bin, and so on until a mail carrier puts it in the recipient's mailbox.

And that's exactly how a network works. The user's modem dials a local telephone number that connects with the network, and then it begins to send data. A local hub computer at the entry point separates the data into packets all the same length and writes the recipient's address, and the sender's return address, into each packet. It puts these packets in with a lot of other packets and sends them to another computer, which reads each packet's address and routes it over a long distance telephone line to a similar computer nearest its destination. This computer reads the address and routes our packet onto a line going directly to the destination computer.

The network's control computers keep track of all these paths and decide instantly which path to use for each packet. For instance, the shortest route from Chicago to New York could run through a switch center in Detroit. But if the Detroit-to-New York line is too crowded, the Detroit center might route the traffic through another center in Atlanta that can provide a clear path all the way to New York. If Atlanta traffic gets heavy, the system might establish a path through Boston.

This process actually takes place in hundredths of a second. With several thousand users sharing each long distance line, the system might send one packet by way of Detroit, the next by way of Denver, the third via Akron, and so on. The packets are all neatly reassembled by the exit computer so the user thinks he is the only one on the line!

SERVICE BUREAUS

The Fortune 500 companies all have their own telecommunications resources. But a lot of medium-sized companies need teleconferencing or voice mail only once in a while.

Service bureaus are available to serve the occasional user. They have voice mail systems, attended teleconference bridges, and other communications facilities, and they charge by the hour. They enable the medium-sized company to use the same efficient techniques the multinationals use, in proportion. In general, a small service bureau will provide the best service to a relatively small company because it offers more personal attention. These small bureaus are often run by technically well informed entrepreneurs who are eager to help. The larger service bureaus can afford the more powerful systems that handle heavy traffic loads at a lower unit cost. Their sales representatives are helpful, but they can devote appreciable time only to companies whose high traffic volume can pay for the powerful systems.

TELEWORK

Cottage industries during the early industrial days paid workers piecework wages to knit garments, address envelopes, and so on, at home. This arrangement offered the companies an advantage in that they didn't have to pay for a building with its utilities and maintenance. Workers didn't have to pay for commuting and office clothing, and could be near their children.

From an economic perspective, the arrangement was efficient. From a social perspective, it was mixed. The unions felt that piecework put too much emphasis on productivity and not enough on job security; the workers effectively were independent subcontractors. This same independence and dispersal of workers made organizing them into a labor movement nearly impossible. The unions had enough clout to suppress cottage industry, and the central work place model became standard.

In the 1990s the sun rises on a different reality. Millions of us dress for work, turn off the lights, lock our attractive homes, and climb into our expensive cars. We inch onto highways so crowded that helicopters fly over them reporting delays, and we converge eventually on a downtown so crowded that parking is an ongoing challenge. Once there, we go into buildings designed to accommodate hundreds of people in productive work. The worker commits perhaps ten hours a day to this effort, although only about eight are actually productive. The worker also pays indirectly, in reduced salary, for building rent, utilities, and maintenance.

Telework, also called telecommuting, allows workers to stay at home, to log onto a terminal connected by telephone lines to a central computer system, and to do the same work previously done in the office. The office's vital information is in digital, rather than in paper, form. The teleworker can research any of it from a remote terminal, modify it as necessary, send it where necessary by electronic mail, receive documents from others online, and generally do whatever else office-based workers do with paper documents.

Meetings are held in three ways: by voice, by data, and in person. A voice teleconference allows any number to "attend" and all to hear one another. An online conference is the digital equivalent; each participant in turn types text all others can read, accepting a slower information transfer rate to get an instant transcript, important when each participant has made commitments to deliver specific products on an agreed schedule. Small gatherings of two or three are usually at restaurants;

teleworkers enjoy getting out once in a while. Large conferences are usually held at a hotel conference facility.

Teleworkers have more control of their lives, since work can often be done any time of the day or evening, although there are "core hours" during which the teleworker is expected to be available. Teleworkers can change jobs more easily by simply logging onto a job bank database right from home, their résumés neatly stored on disk and ready for transmission.

Telework employers get sharply reduced office space costs, partly offset by increased information management costs. They also see more productivity in most cases since teleworking focuses on productivity. Managing a company of teleworkers is different, however. Performance standards closely related to the individual employee's true productivity have to be developed, project management systems have to be instituted, and the whole communication structure has to be defined. These needs force managers to work harder because they can no longer assess performance by observing motion and effort, but productivity assessment, project management, and communications enhancement lead to success in any organization.

Unions oppose teleworking. It is hard to organize teleworkers and even harder to get them to strike. But unions do raise some fair issues. Many workers like the office environment, the social moments. Others encounter problems in the home with work time and space. Some workers lack self-discipline and need to be in a structured environment.

The answer lies in pluralism. Some jobs, as in manufacturing, will never be done from a remote location. Others can be done remotely only in limited circumstances; physicians, for instance, can give advice and monitor patients remotely but will probably always examine and treat patients at a central location using specialized equipment. College instruction is a mixed case—sometimes more effective in a lecture environment and at other times, especially where access to specialists in rare disciplines is necessary, in a remote terminal environment. Probably for decades to come, some senior management teams will be comfortable with the teleworking idea, while others will not. Employees will tend to seek out employers who offer the environment they prefer.

Teleworking is a far-reaching office communications concept. It is extremely efficient for "knowledge workers," but the social patterns required to support it are still evolving. Many companies are experimenting with it gingerly, having some workers telework one day a week, or as necessary. The individual employee's attitude is paramount.

Telework is most common in young, entrepreneurial companies with the on-board brainpower to measure performance by results rather than by appearance of effort; such companies attract star-performer employees seeking a free and creative work environment. Teleworking will spread, a little at a time, throughout the knowledge sector, especially as colleges and universities use it to put faculty and students in contact with specialists around the world, as well as to control the spiraling cost of traditional education.

Each year, as fewer new people enter the work force, companies will compete for the bright young stars. Many will see that teleworking's inherent modularity makes it an attractive option in an increasingly fast-changing and competitive world.

SYSTEM INTEGRATION

Each of these technologies, standing alone, offers excellent results. Major business communication systems, however, often combine them.

Combination can be an economic necessity, as in the intercompany network. One company recognizes the need for an expensive network but blanches at the cost. It sets up the system and sells time on it to other companies in the same business. The airline industry offers a prime example; most of the major airlines and travel agents use either American Airlines's "Sabre" reservation system or United Airlines's competing "Apollo" system.

A combination can also be technology based, as with video teleconferencing. A marriage of the teleconference with video technology, video teleconferencing offers executives in large, multinational corporations an opportunity to meet using visual as well as audible cues without the costs and risks of physical travel. Video teleconference facilities are set up in luxurious conference rooms with overhead cameras and microphones, often with a secretary setting up and controlling the calls, operating a slide projector, and videotaping the proceedings for the record.

The best video teleconference rooms require expensive equipment as well as considerable expertise to set up. A communications expert, an acoustics expert, and a video expert at least are required to work on acoustics, lighting, auxiliary graphic displays, even the conference table. With costly line charges, relatively few companies have installed in-house systems so far. Some hotels have been offering video teleconference facilities so several companies can "share" the cost.

These basic building blocks will be used to implement new business communication systems for the rest of this century. The companies that combine them in the most imaginative ways will have the racer's edge.

INTEGRATED ANALYSIS AND DESIGN

Tom Wolfe wrote that you can't go home again. Home isn't there anymore. Like Brigadoon, it exists only in the mists of memory. Today, there's a four-lane highway where the old cowpath was, and a skyscraper where the old schoolhouse stood. It is not, in the end, a matter of choice.

A company that leased black rotary-dial telephones back in 1950 and still has them, that still uses "office manual" typewriters and carbon paper, would be out of business, its sclerotic communications system unable to match those of competitors using digital-age systems.

Most companies still analyze their communications one compartment at a time. Nearly all the major companies have a mail room supervisor who looks at communication as the physical movement of documents. Many have a telecommunications staff that keeps abreast of their voice and data transmission requirements. Some send their sales representatives to classes on how to talk to clients. Others hire paperwork managers to handle document control and records management. A few hire wardrobe engineers who specialize in communication through clothing.

A company's life is sustained by its overall communication pattern, its sharing of management direction and technical expertise to form interactions that produce new combinations, new ideas, new ways to deliver goods and services. Its communications analyses should be as broad. The objective is to share information so efficiently as to create a virtual "single brain," a oneness of information and experience that is available as needed to every employee—*E pluribus unum.*

Chapter 7

POTPOURRI

We communicate over distances in many ways other than via telephone networks. Each is less important than the telephone network but offers interesting benefits.

THE UNITED STATES POSTAL SERVICE

Benjamin Franklin was the most eloquent among the founding fathers in promoting the idea of a national postal service. He felt the new nation needed a communications network. The idea was accepted, and he became the first postmaster general.

Today, the postal system is a quaint relic. In the technetronic age, when we move information around the world at the speed of light, it still works by physically carrying a piece of paper from one place to another. Bills can now be paid through electronic mail, with each person's computer approving bank payments when amounts are within anticipated ranges. Advertisements, as well as solicitations for political and charitable causes, could be phoned in for display at the user's convenience. Personal correspondence is more practical by phone. The phone offers interaction and can even be less expensive; a person who values the time spent writing a letter at salary rates will find calling more economical.

The United States Postal Service is even going backward. Over the past two decades it has trimmed the size of the overnight delivery zone, slowed more distant delivery, reduced the number of business deliveries per day, pushed for cluster box residential delivery, cut back on pickups, all while increasing the cost of first-class mail much faster than the rate of inflation.

But the old communications dinosaur trudges on. From ocean to ocean and door to door, it picks up mail, sorts mail, and delivers mail, because sometimes a dinosaur comes in handy.

As long as electronic identification codes are vulnerable to surreptitious alteration, a document with an ink signature will still be the *sine qua non* for legal validity. Americans put more emphasis on legal instruments and legal process than any other nation on Earth. It is a lot easier to tap a phone line than a sealed letter.

Also, we have international postal treaties and, hence, responsibilities. Electronic data bits moving hither and yon at the speed of light are feasible in the United States, Japan, and Western Europe, but are less so in sparsely populated countries like Canada or Australia, and a lost cause in the third world. We can't conscientiously withdraw from an established international communication system.

Besides, the post office is familiar. The rate of change in electronic communications has been incredible over the past decade. Such common items as mobile and portable telephones, line features, and public information utilities scarcely existed ten years ago. Although many "knowledge sector" people revel in the new options, many others feel a sense of vertigo. Erich Fromm's *Escape from Freedom* chronicled the surprisingly common fear of choice, the fear of error, twenty-five years ago. For these people, the postal system offers easy communication with faraway relatives.

COMMERCIAL RADIO

Land Mobile

Land mobile communications are personal communications used in a vehicle or on foot. Police, fire, ambulance, and other public service agencies use land mobile radio to communicate with one another and with "central." Public bus transit companies use it to coordinate service. Phrases like "See the woman at ... ," "Apartment on fire at ... ," "Collision with injuries at ... ," "I have a breakdown—please send backup bus to ... ," travel over these systems constantly. Taxi drivers, television repair technicians, tow truck operators, heating and air conditioning service specialists, and countless others use land mobile radio to coordinate their daily business activities.

Service organizations with small coverage areas, such as rescue squads, just put their "base station" radio antenna on a tall tower at the headquarters building and have "line of sight" radio coverage throughout their jurisdiction. But that arrangement wouldn't work for municipal or county police departments—they place a repeater in each area where they need radio coverage. A repeater is nothing more than an automatic relay station that retransmits signals.

The oldest repeaters were neighborhood gossips. Over the centuries they have broadcast information about daily life within their communities. Despite its low reliability, this type of repeater is still popular today.

After beacon fires, at least, the first real advances in repeater technology were the old semaphores and shutter telegraphs, where a message was visually relayed from one station to the next. The Toulon and Paris stations couldn't see one another, just as the New York and Philadelphia stations couldn't see each other, so they communicated through intermediate stations that could see one another. Now suppose old George Murray had found a way to place just one shutter telegraph relay station on a mile-high tower in central New Jersey and had used very powerful telescopes. The relay tower would then have operated as a visual repeater.

Modern radio repeaters are mounted on tall building roofs, mountaintops, or commercial towers. A basic repeater just sits on its high perch. Its receiver is set on a particular channel, and anything it hears is fed straight into its transmitter and re-broadcast from above the hills and buildings that would otherwise block the reliable "line of sight" radio frequencies. A municipal police officer anywhere within the repeater's coverage area can thus talk to any other officer. But the police department, from its downtown headquarters building, has to be able to talk to all its officers, even though its jurisdiction extends over several repeater coverage areas. So it leases a line from the telephone company for use twenty-four hours a day between each of its repeaters and the headquarters communications center. The dispatcher can then control each repeater and be in contact with everyone at the same time.

A single network of repeaters might be enough for a municipal police department, but what about a major state or federal law enforcement agency? Each of its regional headquarters is apt to have a radio communications center, with repeaters connected by leased telephone lines to the regional center.

The Lonely Crowd

The radio spectrum is a constant—you can only make better use of the bands you have claim to or take someone else's. However, the number of people who want to use the radio spectrum increases geometrically. Parson Malthus would have understood.

Making better use of a band is expensive. It often means scrapping existing equipment and buying newer equipment with narrower channels so more channels fit into the band. Taking someone else's band is less expensive for the taker, because someone else loses out. To persuade the political system that new channels are needed, a user has to argue that his existing channel is crowded—for example, the field people have to wait ten minutes just to get a short message through, and so forth. This process leads a lot of people to exaggerate, since the one who tells the biggest tale gets more spectrum.

There are better ways to decide allocations. Special scanners exist today that can sample 10,000 radio channels very rapidly and note whether on any given scan a particular channel is in use. Running several of these scans at different times of day, different days of the week, and so on, will show very accurately what percent of time a channel is in use. A channel in use forty seconds an hour is busy 1 percent of the time; if in use six minutes every hour, it is busy 10 percent of the time.

Standards can be set by the Federal Communications Commission as to what levels of use are acceptable. Large companies could then buy these scanners to measure their own use levels, and they could then file requests for more space only when the need is confirmed by objective measurement. Smaller companies could turn to independent firms for these measurements.

AMATEUR RADIO

Amateur radio is a worldwide hobby of personal communication. It is controlled by international treaty and regulated by each country's national government. Amateur radio operators have to pass rigorous exams in radio theory and rules of operation before they can be licensed.

The examinations stand guard at the gates of the amateur fraternity, admitting only those whose technical knowledge is sufficient to assure responsible use of their remarkable privileges. They also admit individuals who care enough for the hobby to become proficient in radio communication and who will study the regulations enough to understand them. Anyone can be an amateur radio operator—farmers, bankers, carpenters, doctors, housewives, engineers, writers, repair technicians, students, artists, professors, inspectors, weather forecasters, and many more add color and interest to the amateur community.

Astronaut Owen Garriott, an amateur radio operator, spoke with hundreds of ordinary folks from the space shuttle while orbiting 175 miles above the Earth. He credits amateur radio with arousing his interest in electronics and the space program. King Hussein of Jordan, too, is an active and expert amateur radio operator. His many friends just call him "Hussein" and treat him like anyone else. He talks about his cars, skiing, his friends' children, and life. In fact, during the 1970 civil war in Jordan, the capital city of Amman was sealed; even the wire services couldn't get a word in or out. A tense Hussein turned to amateur radio, and his friends all over the world engaged him in diverting conversation.

Amateur radio operators ask Scandinavians how they live with ice and snow, Colombians how they beat the heat, Swiss how they keep their country so neat and their railroads so punctual. They ask Italians about La Scala in Milan and the canals in Venice and the Vatican in Rome. They ask Australians about the Sydney opera house, about kangaroos, koalas, and the outback. They ask Japanese about the Akhihabara section of Tokyo. They ask Hawaiians about the forbidden island of Niihau. They ask Iowa farmers about wheat. The most daring even ask Texans about chili.

Another intriguing aspect of amateur radio is that someone else is always listening; quite often amateurs will tune in to listen rather than to talk. In general, conversations are about what you'd expect at a social gathering: what you do for a living, where you come from, and so on, although some will discuss such flammable subjects as sex, religion, and politics if there is mutual respect and sensitivity.

Amateurs can also work with television on their ultra high frequency bands. There are some very normal people who, after hours, go upstairs into a hobby room. They turn on their TV receivers, aim their TV cameras at themselves, and check into the local amateur television group. They introduce their spouses, kids, and pooches to their friends. They play chess, show off their computer graphics, talk about the local schools, and create new frontiers in personal communication.

Emergencies bring amateurs out in force. In a major blizzard, earthquake, hurricane, airline crash, railroad collision, or other disaster, mobile and portable communications are critical to mobilize needed help and to find out which hospitals are prepared to handle what injuries and patient loads. When police, sheriffs, fire fighters, and paramedics all converge, the mutual aid channels get crowded to the point of chaos. What's more, rescuers have to spend their precious time saving lives, not trying to get a word in edgewise. Amateurs who are trained in disaster communications then move in with approval from local authorities and provide the vital information exchange.

Even amateur radio technology has some romance in it. Long distance conversations follow the curve of the Earth by bouncing off the ionosphere as a flat stone skips over water. The high frequency bands used for these contacts are sometimes "open" to 10,000 mile conversations. Amateur operators sail the airwaves; they ride an open band until it weakens and then artfully change to one that is getting stronger.

There is romance above the ionosphere, too. Amateur radio operators have their own communications satellites, so that line-of-sight radio signals can be used for overseas contacts. The amateurs who build these satellites are usually aerospace engineers who work on them evenings and weekends. On their own time, these engineers pursue cost-saving ideas for their satellites. To foster this activity, the aerospace firms and NASA allow amateurs to share space on rockets launching commercial or government satellites. Everyone benefits; NASA and the aerospace companies get free research, while the amateurs get another little repeater that whirls around the planet every two hours or so.

INFORMATION UTILITIES

Information utilities let consumers call up computer

news, encyclopedia articles, stock prices, mutual fund ratings, ski conditions, and car prices. They allow transactions such as home shopping, banking, airline and hotel booking, and bill paying. They provide electronic mail and online conferences with others who share virtually every kind of interest.

To sit at home in front of a personal computer and log onto a remote database is like Keats's first look into Chapman's Homer. There is a sense of limitless knowledge and power. The user can peruse vast areas of information, like an eagle soaring high over the land, and can then dive in, precisely on target. Want to know what flights to Honolulu are available and to book tickets? Want to know what's been published this year about General Motors's quality control? Just ask.

Information utilities are starting to become familiar in the "knowledge community." The handicapped are finding some advantages. The blind, for instance, can use speech synthesizers to hear data as "spoken" words, or they can send the text to a Braille printer.

So far, most people have bought information in book-size quantities or less. The largest source of information available in an integrated package is the Encyclopedia Britannica. Little silver disks—Compact Disk Read Only Memory (CD-ROM's)—which store text and other formatted data, have been called "the new papyrus" because their storage density exceeds that of paper as much as paper's storage density eclipsed markings on rock.

A single disk can store all the great works of English

literature. Another could store all the doctoral theses ever written in the United States in an entire discipline. A third could hold the entire news content of *The New York Times* for a year. A fourth could hold all of the census data for a decade, while a fifth could hold the *Encyclopedia of Religion and Ethics,* the *Interpreter's Bible,* the *New Catholic Encyclopedia,* and the *Encyclopedia Judaica.* A sixth could store a street map of the United States. The disks allow formidable amounts of research, with personal computers programmed to search through indexes or the entire disk to hunt down specific information.

But CD-ROM will not replace the online database as a source for fast-changing information. The user who wants to check on the latest medical research, or the one who wants to know what flights have seats available tomorrow morning, or what the stock market did within the past fifteen minutes, will have to find the information online.

Nor will it replace the book. Books are user-friendly, portable, random-access, and easy on the eyes. Information utilities and CD-ROM convey facts and statistics well, but books are still the best way to move a concept from one mind to another.

DISCREET INFORMATION: HOW THE KGB DOES IT

"Discretion," Falstaff said, "is the better part of valor." The KGB, in its continuing efforts to acquire United States military and technological information, lives by that maxim.

Ordinary discreet communications, say the kind used to arrange love in the afternoon, are of interest primarily to spouses or office snoops. The KGB's mission requires that it communicate, without appearing to do so, under the watchful eyes of trained federal investigators.

Its most common method is the dead-drop. A KGB handler puts prearranged graffiti or chalk strokes on a lamppost or trash can. When the agent spots the graffiti or chalk strokes, the handler puts his instructions, always coded and sometimes on a microdot or microfilm, in a magnetic capsule called a limpet. He attaches this late at night to the lamppost or an elevated subway pillar, bridge pillar, movie theater seat, or other opportune spot, and leaves the area, often by public transportation. A short time later, the agent arrives and retrieves the limpet.

Sometimes an agent has information for his handler that cannot readily be reduced, like a bulky technical manual. In such instances, the two show up somewhere with identical attaché cases. Without acknowledging one another's presence, both put their cases down, perhaps fish out some change to buy a hot dog from a street vendor, "accidentally" pick up one another's cases, and move on.

More of this action goes on in New York City than anywhere else. The United Nations still has a lot of KGB operatives on its payroll. New York also has a lot of elevated subway pillars, lampposts, pay phones, and graffiti. The subways run all night and provide anonymous transportation.

Washington, D.C., is another hot spot. The new Soviet

embassy on Mt. Alto, the third highest elevation in the nation's capital, is well situated to pick up long distance telephone conversations carried by microwave, as well as being in line of sight to the White House, the CIA building, the Pentagon, and the State Department. The embassy has a large array of receiving antennas concealed on its top floor and a powerful computer that picks out the interesting conversations, based on originating and receiving telephone numbers. The embassy staff is larger than that required for traditional diplomatic business. A lot of information moves in and out of the nation's capital, and some of it gets intercepted.

Chapter 8

THE LIBERAL ARTS

Literature, music, and art provide a common experience from which allusions can be drawn. They also communicate cultural values from one generation to the next.

As information transmission becomes more and more efficient, the tendency to overload each individual in the "knowledge sector" becomes endemic. Each of us must develop the ability to filter information input so that the useful comes through while the extraneous is never seen. The liberal arts are comments on the human condition by some of the most perceptive and articulate people on Earth. Consider Robert Frost's, "Something there is that doesn't love a wall," a cogent remark about personal decisions. The blind might find ideas worth considering in the pages of John Milton, or the person going deaf can listen once more to Beethoven's *Eroica* for an appropriate attitude toward the coming silence.

We sometimes reserve time for Shakespeare but not

for Congreve, time for Bach but not for Lully, but in doing so we take a calculated risk. Great writers, musicians, and artists are particularly sensitive. Some are effervescent, like Mozart, others courageous, like Beethoven. They have in common the ability to reflect the human condition with extraordinary accuracy so that we recognize ourselves in their work. As Balzac said: "Art is nature concentrated."

LITERATURE

Literature helps us communicate by compressing cultural experience into a few words. When we read the great novels, for instance, we store their vistas in memory.

American novels, appropriately enough, reflect life in America. We often dream of the legendary "great American novel" in which the entire spirit of the land is caught. But life is wider than any one observer's ken; the great American novel has been coming out for more than a century now, its chapters written by Edward Bellamy, Saul Bellow, Stephen Crane, Theodore Dreiser, William Faulkner, Nathaniel Hawthorne, Ernest Hemingway, Henry James, Sinclair Lewis, Herman Melville, James Michener, Joyce Carol Oates, Mark Twain, John Updike, Herman Wouk, and many other storytellers from every part of the country.

Great wine, as it matures, absorbs the subtle characteristics of the cask. Men and women too, over the years, absorb and reflect vast experience. When we address the subject of mankind, the depth and range of what we want to communicate would take far too long to express, were it not for the concentrated perspective in novels, plays, and stories. So instead of articulating our ideas in long form, we use novels and other works of fiction as little capsules.

For example, let us attend a performance of *Hamlet*. We see the intelligent, sensitive, well-intentioned young prince confronted by a terrifying experience. Under extreme pressure, Hamlet becomes his opposite—at once indecisive and ruthless—and causes several violent deaths. The shared experience of Shakespeare's vision allows us to wrap this extremely complex persona in the short phrase: "Hamletlike."

T. S. Eliot believed that the most effective way for a writer to communicate with his readers is through what he called the "objective correlative," objective information. Edgar Allan Poe's *A Cask of Amontillado* doesn't just say the man behind the wall was frightened. The protagonist describes how, while his adversary was in a drunken stupor in the wine cellar, he put him in a far corner and built a wall brick by brick until, with the last brick in place, he had built a small "room" with no door, no window, no light, no sound, no fresh air. We have enough objective information then to envision the entombed man during his transition from stupor to reality. We share his groping for an exit, his hands exploring for a tiny opening, his nose inhaling the damp, stagnant air, his ears hearing only the sound of his own movements, and his eyes seeing nothing at all.

Literary works help people communicate in another way. Men and women are often reluctant to discuss their own relationships. Sometimes the relationship is so precious to them that putting it into words defines and limits it. In other situations the relationship might depend on an exchange of services that neither wishes to acknowledge openly. Many men and women communicate about relationships by taking one another to see plays that reflect their lives.

MUSIC

The term "music" comes from the Greek legends of Mount Olympus, where nine charming goddesses, called Muses, sang while Apollo accompanied on the lyre. Music is tone in patterns of sensuous beauty. Below the surface, it transmits emotional information from composer to listener.

Music involves a relation between musician and listener. At Bayreuth, for instance, when *Die Walküre* is played, each listener's mind drifts during the Ride of the Valkyries. One listener swells with pride in the German spirit as Brünnhilde carries the fallen warriors off to Valhalla; another notices the interplay of leitmotifs and compares it with the interplay of characters. The physical, emotional, and intellectual elements are interwoven in the bond between musician and listener.

Traditional music is the only art form that uses an interpreter between the original artist and the audience. Stravinsky said, for instance, that the tempo toward the end of *Firebird* must be "as steady as a heartbeat." But a heartbeat changes tempo as excitement mounts. The performer decides whether Stravinsky meant as steady as a metronome. The musical idea communicated to the listener, then, comes already translated.

The power of suggestion in music is formidable. Just for fun, Enrico Caruso once sang Beppe's offstage serenade in the second act of *Pagliacci* and only got that mild applause usually given to the minor singers who normally play Beppe, although his onstage performance as Canio drew thunderous acclamation. Most in the audience did not realize who had sung the serenade and were applauding by reputation.

Music, by that power of suggestion, can transport a listener across time and distance as can no other medium. Noel Coward wrote in *Private Lives,* "Strange how potent cheap music is." When we listen to the music of our childhood years, we are there again, just for a while.

But music can do even more. Pete Seeger used to sing a wonderful song, *"God Bless the Grass,"* about the grass that grew through the cracks of city sidewalks. Its allegorical message was that the more ideas are repressed, the more they push through the cracks. It was the urban expression of "Something there is that doesn't love a wall," and a distant echo of John Donne.

And more than that: During the Civil War, every evening at sundown, the Union Army bugler with each unit played "Taps." Confederate soldiers, listening from across the battlefields, also felt its serene reassurance. After a while, their buglers, too, played "Taps" at sundown. "Taps," as it echoed in the hills from army to army, formed a sort of bond between the opposing troops.

And still more. At the opera house one night, the lights in the great chandelier dim and finally go dark. The orchestra plays the thirty-one bars of music that introduce *La Bohème,* and the curtain opens onto Rodolfo and Marcello in a garret. Puccini has already begun communicating a narrative with an underlying sense that love transcends circumstances. This subliminal message is so effective that Harry Golden once warned young men, "Never take a girl to see *La Bohème* unless you want to marry her."

Does the audience communicate back to the musicians? Listen after each aria to see whether the applause rises gradually to a polite level or explodes into a torrent. Claques leave tracks. At curtain call time, the cries of "bravo" for the tenor and the flowers flung to the soprano are real if they match enthusiasm in the applause, counterfeit if they appear to be driving it.

The performers understand well enough, and they answer plainly. Singers know how to smile and pretend to appreciate even weak applause, but the real McCoy puts a twinkle in their eyes and spring in their movements.

ART

Art is music for the eyes. Its categories include architecture, painting, photography, and sculpture.

A work of art communicates an original idea or a well-known idea from a new angle. Consider Picasso's *Bull's Head,* which consists only of a bicycle saddle and handlebars. The saddle is positioned vertically, the front part down to resemble an animal's nose and the rear part up to resemble the wider, upper part of the head. The handlebars are attached to the back of the saddle facing up, to resemble horns. Common materials—but so placed they communicate, and provide evidence for, an idea: There is order and symmetry on Earth, and even things that seem disparate are in fact linked.

Communicating cultural values is much more than walking around a museum of art and gazing upon a Rembrandt. The prophet Mohammed went to his reward in the year 632, leaving behind a faith that, like Christianity, was an offshoot of Judaism. The Jews, seeing themselves as the chosen people, never went after converts. Their central statement, the Shema, was proclaimed in the synagogues: "Hear, oh *Israel*, the Lord our God, the Lord is one!" Mohammedans, however, equally sure they had the one true faith, opened it to all mankind. Five times a day, the muezzin climbed into his minaret and called out: "Hark ye, *all men!* God is great. There is no god but God and Mohammed is the only prophet of God."

Reflecting this difference, early mosques were very different from the synagogues and churches of the day. They were not holy, because no god lived inside. Desert worshipers, accustomed to living in tents, had no need of benches or chairs and were happy to squat on the floor. The mosque had four walls, a roof, a niche in one wall to indicate the direction to Mecca, and a pulpit. But Islamic architecture sent a powerful message. Every mosque had a fountain of running water in which the faithful were to wash before entering. People who live on the desert see water as life. The symbolism worked, and people came from all over.

The Alhambra in Granada, Spain, and the Notre Dame Cathedral in Paris show how architecture communicates. The contrast between the Alhambra's ordinary, unassuming exterior and the richly decorated interior conveys a sense that Islam's true beauty is only apparent to the faithful. There is water everywhere, usually in basins or fountains. The slim columns or windowed walls supporting heavy, elaborately decorated ceilings suggest that people who band together in one faith can do more than might seem apparent. The cupolas are symbolic domes of heaven revolving around the prince sitting under them.

Notre Dame, by contrast, has great vertical lines and structures to suggest reaching upward toward God. Its interior appears to be high, airy, and weightless, suggesting heaven above. Its sheer size suggests power and permanence.

A walk through either the Alhambra or Notre Dame communicates to the perceptive observer a sense of the Islamic or Catholic faith that cannot be conveyed in words.

Chapter 9

EXTRASENSORY COMMUNICATION

Science today is the regnant means of acquiring and communicating information about the world around us, the senior warden at the gates of knowledge. However, the inquiring mind will retain a healthy skepticism. Modern physics, for instance, no longer accepts that an atom is like a hard billiard ball; it is more like a ballroom where dancers move at random. Subatomic particles move, change direction, and spin in unpredictable ways, unlike anything we know. Some particles appear to act on one another instantaneously at extreme distances. Others might never be detectable because they exist in a zone of uncertainty. The probability of a given behavior can be computed, but the time and location of the behavior cannot. Yet, quantum mechanics is essential to modern technology from biochemistry to semiconductors, and even to an understanding of gravity. Both of the revolutions in physics—the first was mechanics; the second, relativity and quantum theory—exposed as shallow the orthodoxy of centuries. The wise observer has an open mind.

151

Moreover, scientific disciplines do not progress at a uniform rate. Physics is far advanced; we can send a man to the moon and return him safely to the Earth because we can predict very accurately how his spacecraft will behave. Medicine is less advanced; we can swap hearts but are just learning to cure the common cold.

Parapsychology is a science, but it is behind the established sciences because there are a lot of charlatans in the field. First-rate scientists are reluctant to work among charlatans.

It is kept rather quiet, but both the United States and the Soviet Union have psychic warfare programs. For instance, clairvoyance, the ability to describe scenes thousands of miles away, was used by the CIA on a project called "Grill Flame." A psychic was given the latitude and longitude of a remote location and asked to describe the scene. He described an airfield in considerable detail, including a large gantry and crane at one end of the field.

The CIA was impressed. The site was the Soviets' ultrasecret nuclear testing area at Semipalatinsk, Kazakhstan, although United States satellite photos showed no gantry or crane. Since the photos were not that recent, the CIA waited for the next set of satellite photos and saw the gantry and crane exactly as described. No one in United States intelligence had known they were there.

There have been other extraordinary instances of clairvoyance and tests of other kinds. Obviously, the ability to gather intelligence by remote viewing would allow psychics on either side to read the other side's most secret documents, diagrams, or blueprints. Still, the Pentagon is reportedly spending only about one million dollars a year for exploration of the potential capabilities of the human mind.

The Soviets take extrasensory communication much more seriously. The CIA estimates they are spending about seventy million dollars a year on research into extrasensory communication and psychokinesis at fourteen laboratories in Moscow and at least ten others in other Soviet cities. They hope to affect the heartbeat and respiration of faraway victims and already claim to have had some success.

Some kind of communication certainly occurs independently of the traditional five senses, so we will explore it, recognizing the primitive condition of our tools but searching the uncharted territory for new insight into our links with one another. Pope reminds us: "The proper study of mankind is man."

WHAT IT IS

We are all surrounded by invisible waves carrying information to and from every corner of the Earth. Electromagnetic waves carry radio and television signals to the eyes and ears of every man, woman, and child. Special devices, invented in this century, show them to us. Extrasensory communication depends on a real world medium that science has not yet discovered.

Telepathy is sending or receiving information by direct

thought; it is independent of distance and is said to occur both among the living and between the living and the departed. Clairvoyance is receiving an image of remote persons, objects, or events, as in Project Grill Flame. Precognition is movement of information across time, from future to present, in other words, knowing about specific events before they occur. Sometimes precognition is experienced in retrospect as déjà vu. Retrocognition, its counterpart, is the movement of information from past to present, or knowing about specific events of the past by extrasensory means. It sometimes shows up when people describe past lives, giving information later corroborated by researchers.

The human brain, composed of two hemispheres, depends on an attraction of opposites, a mutual dependency, a restless series of confrontations creating an endless stream of new combinations. The usually dominant left hemisphere is the brain's arithmetic-logic unit; it organizes ideas into spoken and written words, calculates timing, and does other rational analysis. The right hemisphere handles recognition of faces and images, creative expression, love, appreciation of beauty, enjoyment of music, and intuition. Two entirely separate personalities in the same skull, communicating constantly with one another so that the two work together as one without conscious effort. Extrasensory communication, probably handled somewhere in the convoluted neurons of the more subtle right brain, might be the most efficient communications transceiver on Earth.

We can speculate about how extrasensory communication might work. The Einstein-Podolsky-Rosen paradox says that if two particles move apart at the speed of light and an experimenter changes the direction of one particle, the second particle will alter its course as well. There must be some energy field, some medium, through which "information" about one particle is transmitted to the other.

British mathematician Adrian Dobbs suggested that the world of subatomic particles might point the way to a coherent theory of extrasensory perception. He proposed the existence of subatomic particles called "psitrons" that, like neutrinos, travel in swarms and have only imaginary mass. Such psitrons would be too small to encounter resistance and therefore would keep going until detected by receptors in the brain.

Another theory is that a parallel universe exists in the same physical space as ours but in a different dimension. At some level, usually subconscious, we can communicate through it. Perhaps psitrons are transdimensional. That universe would be noncorporeal, accounting for experimental evidence that accuracy in telepathy and clairvoyance are independent of distance, and would be timeless, accounting for precognition and retrocognition. When we say a person has "passed on," it may be to this parallel universe, accounting for reports of contact with the departed.

Rupert Sheldrake in his book, *A New Science of Life,* asserted that once some members of a group learn a given task, others can tap their knowledge through a "morphogenetic field" to learn it more easily. Most tests of the morphic resonance theory to date have been inconclusive, but a few carefully conducted tests show some interesting correlations. In one, a professor at New

York University had a group of Yale students who did not know Hebrew look at a set of three-letter words. Half were real Hebrew words, the rest random Hebrew characters. The students then guessed the meanings and rated their confidence in each guess. The results showed that students were significantly more confident at guessing the meaning of real words, and most confident of the most frequently used words. The morphogenetic field might be a parallel universe; the research continues.

Arthur Koestler wrote in *The Roots of Coincidence:* "At least these theories, based on assumptions which sound weird but hardly more weird than those of modern physics, go a long way toward removing the aura of superstition from the 'extra' in extrasensory perception. The odour of the alchemist's kitchen is replaced by the smell of quark in the laboratory."

Whatever the mechanics, there certainly is extrasensory communication going on. In one well-documented instance, Edgar Cayce in 1937 did a life reading for a woman. He told her that two thousand years ago she had been an Essene, and that the Essenes had a house of study on the shores of the Dead Sea. Cayce told her the Essenes preserved sacred writings by copying them, studying them, and teaching them to the young. The recopied scrolls were stored in alabaster jars. When Jerusalem fell, the monastery was attacked. To save their work, he told her, the Essenes hid the alabaster jars in nearby mountain caves.

About ten years after Cayce gave this reading, an Arab boy playing in a mountain cave came upon some alabaster jars. He opened them and took out some chips of parchment. The boy didn't recognize the strange writing, but he brought them back to his village. Eventually, scholars in Jerusalem recognized the chips for what they were, went to the cave, and there discovered the Dead Sea Scrolls.

THE HUMAN AURA

The human aura has been described as a colorful energy field around the body that mirrors a person's physical, mental, and emotional condition and is putatively visible to us all at the subconscious level. Probably we evolved these colors in harmony with nature. Fire and blood are red. Sunlight, which illuminates the Earth, is often seen as yellow. The trees and grass that recover each spring from the icy gray of winter are mostly green. The sky, the legendary home of the Deity in so many civilizations, is blue.

Auras are controversial. Few people consciously see them. Apparently, those who do see them tend to be intensely "visual" people such as artists rather than the verbal types such as academics, and even among intensely visual types only the few who are open and receptive actually register them at the conscious level. Of those who do see auras, most use their gift without ever telling anyone, not even their own spouses. Business managers concerned about political intrigue might "read" their associates for signs of their true intentions. Negotiators could read whether the other side has actually given its rock bottom offer. Sales representatives, as they talk, could observe a prospect's unspoken reactions. Professional gamblers would see whether even the most "poker-faced" opponent is pleased with his or her cards.

Even among the tiny minority who brave skepticism and openly say that they see auras, most live and die recognized for their gifts only in the small towns or local neighborhoods in which they live and read for their friends. Only a few persons have written books so that others might share their insights.

Of course, we must separate the wheat from the chaff. In the 1970s, for instance, there was a vogue for Kirlian photography in which the subject was placed between two electrodes and subjected to an electrical field fluctuating up to 200,000 times per second. The electric charges produced blue, violet, and ultraviolet light that exposed the film, but the resulting corona was apparently just a field of transpired water vapor that was ionized.

Some people learned a visual trick to "see" auras. It consisted of staring at a person until the image faded and then shifting vision very slightly. Following this shift, after-images appeared as a result of tiring the optic nerve and retinal retention. The color of the after-image was ordinarily the "complement" to the color of the person being stared at, although a few intensely visual people seem to project the subconsciously seen auric color onto it. This technique can easily be observed by trying it with an inanimate object of any chromatic (not black, gray, or white) color.

Still, even after these disproved cases are eliminated, there remains a core of intriguing evidence. The reports of several persons, such as Edgar Cayce, Ray Stanford, and others, are startlingly consistent with one another, with cave art in Africa and Australia from tens of thousands of years ago, with ancient religious traditions, and with modern reflections such as traffic lights and idiomatic expressions. Perhaps auras will follow acupuncture into wider acceptance, but meanwhile the evidence should persuade an objective observer that *something,* probably seen at the subconscious level by most people, is there.

The Old Testament recounts that Moses, after forty days on Mt. Sinai with God, came down with the second set of commandments, written in stone, and that his face radiated beams of light. Exodus 34:30 says: "And when Aaron and all the children of Israel saw Moses, behold, the skin of his face shone; and they were afraid to come nigh him."

The great sculptor Michelangelo created his beautiful and reverent statue of Moses with horns. The original Hebrew text of Exodus 34:30, more literally translated, says: "... the skin of his face sent forth beams...." The Hebrew word *karnaim* means "beams," but the same word also means "horns." Rashi, the authoritative Old Testament scholar and commentator, notes that this particular word was chosen deliberately, "for the light glistened and projected like a horn." Bibles in Michelangelo's day contained some errors of translation, and this was one. The horns that contribute so much to the statue's sense of *terribilita* are understood by scholars today as symbolic rays.

From early Christian times, saintly persons have been represented in paintings with golden halos. The earliest ones depict a series of lines radiating uniformly from the head, which was later represented as a simple elliptical ring of light.

What the Colors Mean

Red in an aura is said to reflect force, energy, anger, stress, and sexual arousal. We say of persons enveloped by fury that they "see red." On every continent, red is used to warn of danger and to stop traffic at intersections when it would be dangerous to proceed. Houses of ill repute often display a red light in the window.

White is the color of holiness; Edgar Cayce believed that Jesus Christ had an aura of pure white. Pink is the color of children. Pregnant women are said to show pink in the womb area, and young children are said to show it about the entire body. Pink is a mixture of red and white, suggesting that children combine an abundance of energy and glory. We sometimes speak of a person in such a happy condition as "in the pink." Wordsworth offered an explanation for the white part of a child's aura in his "Ode on the Intimations of Immortality." He suggested that the human soul comes from heaven, so we are born "trailing clouds of glory" which slowly fade as we grow up.

Orange in an aura shows ego, and intense pure orange suggests excessive ego. A golden orange indicates euphoria, while a brownish orange points to a lack of ambition.

Yellow is the auric color of intellect. It is the brightest

color, and we speak of an intelligent person as "bright." Children often describe one of their peers as "yellow" if he is inclined to think before acting. All countries use amber, a darker yellow, as the traffic signal indicating "proceed with caution."

Gold is said to be the auric color of the loving, caring person. We say such persons have a "heart of gold." Love and caring were the hallmarks of the early Christian saints.

Green in an aura is the color of healing. Excellent doctors and nurses are said to have pure green in their auras, as are good mothers of young children. Green is used all over the world as the traffic signal for "safe to proceed." However, if an aura tends toward chartreuse, a mixture of green and yellow, the person is pretending to be helpful but is also calculating; chartreuse is said to be the color of deceit. We speak of a person being "green with envy," but usually picture it as chartreuse.

Blue is said to be the auric color of the spirit, of contemplation and inspiration. A deep blue aura suggests a beautiful soul. Freemasons for centuries have identified their quest for the spirit of man with blue and even today refer to their most important work as "blue Masonry." A very light blue aura is said to suggest little depth but a struggle toward maturity. We sometimes say a person is "feeling blue" at such times.

Violet is the auric color of the seeker; it marks a strong drive to reach a goal. When we want something very much, we sometimes say we want it "with a purple passion."

The Kennedy Center for the Performing Arts in Washington, D.C., offers an intriguing opportunity to observe color preferences. In the Hall of Nations are displayed most of the national banners of the civilized world. Most national flags have two colors, generally red, blue, green, or yellow. When one color dominates a flag, the color is most likely red, except in African countries where green—the color of Islam—predominates. In the Hall of Flags appear the fifty American state flags. Most striking is that the northern states, especially the more socially conservative, tend to show lots of blue and green; the sunbelt flags tend toward red and yellow. These effects are also consistent with auric observations. Red and orange are associated with ebullience, with a reaching out to others. The blue and green types can be as happy with just a few intimate friends.

Physical Reactions

The human body responds to color in physical, as well as psychological, ways. Red, orange, and yellow, the "warm" or "hard" colors, actually increase our blood pressure, pulse rate, respiration rate, autonomic nervous activity, and digestion. Green is somewhat neutral in its physical effect although it is classed with blue and violet among the "cool" or "soft" colors. Blue and violet tend to reduce these physical responses.

Red, orange, and yellow are also known as "advancing colors." Red especially is only slightly refracted by the lens of the human eye, and hence focuses at a point behind the retina. In order to see it clearly the eye lens grows more convex, thus pulling the color forward and making the image clearer and larger. Blue, and especially violet, the "receding colors," have the opposite effect. They are refracted enough by the eye lens to focus at a point in front of the retina; the lens responds to a broad field of blue or violet by becoming less convex, thus bringing it into sharp focus on the retina at a greater apparent distance.

Color has a strong effect on the appetite, too. Most of the good things to eat are red, orange, or yellow; these are the colors of meat and fresh fruits such as oranges and bananas. The green foods are all fresh vegetables. There are no blue foods in nature except blueberries. The only purple foods are grapes and grape juice. Probably as a result of associations written deeply into human genes, research indicates that red-orange most stimulates the appetite, followed by red or orange or yellow separately. Blue-green comes next, perhaps from the association with open water fishing in good weather. Green comes after that. Blue is generally neutral. Violet reduces the appetite somewhat, and chartreuse reduces the appetite significantly. Notice the colors associated with such fast-food chains as McDonald's and Hardee's; just driving by sends the message: "Come eat!"

BEYOND THE VEIL

When the first of a pair of twins in the womb is born, it must appear to the second that the first has "passed away." Perhaps it is the same when a soul departs from a body no longer needed and passes on.

Raymond Moody's *Life After Life* chronicles the experiences of people who were resuscitated after having been considered clinically dead by their physicians. Dr. Moody discovered that certain descriptions recurred again and again among people who had no knowledge of one another and were from very different cultural backgrounds.

At first, the soul or consciousness is reported to experience a loud unpleasant buzzing sound as it departs from the physical body and passes through a long, dark tunnel or void. Then the consciousness is said to hover above the body, looking down at it in a state of emotional upheaval. Then it sees the spirits of friends and relatives who have already passed on and have come to help. The presence of a loving warm being who appears to be made of light is reported. After that, a final barrier is said to be noticed, at which point the subjects are turned back to be reunited with their bodies.

Among all the elements in that composite, the single most consistently reported is the being of light. Dr. Moody writes, "Not one person has expressed any doubt whatsoever that it was a being, a being of light."

The accounts relate that, shortly after appearing, the being begins to communicate with the consciousness. The process is invariably described as direct transfer of thoughts. There are no words and no possibility of misunderstanding or lying to the light. The light is described as asking, "Are you prepared?" and "What have you done with your life to show me?" The questions are always described as gentle, warm, and loving.

Dr. Elizabeth Kübler-Ross conducted similar studies with astonishingly similar results, although she did not meet Dr. Moody until both had completed their books. At this point, the studies have been publicized enough that further studies could be influenced by suggestion. But the remarkable coincidence of reports before the publicity indicates that there could be an afterlife. There is some evidence of communication between the living and the departed.

Mrs. Rosemary Brown, a British woman with no musical inclination, claimed that world-class composers—Beethoven, Brahms, and Schubert—were dictating musical scores to her, which she wrote down. Experts agreed that they may have been genuine; the scores were characteristic of the respective composers, were of high quality, and would have taken exceptional talent to produce. Why these composers might have chosen Mrs. Brown over someone like Arturo Toscanini is not clear, unless they wanted their names associated with the scores and felt everyone would believe Toscanini had written them. In any case, the facts are a matter of record and there is no obvious explanation.

Adela Rogers St. Johns, who covered the major news stories of the mid-twentieth century for the Hearst chain, wrote *No Good-Byes* "to express my conviction, based on undeniable experience, that life is indeed eternal." "Based on undeniable experience"; what a striking phrase from the pen of a professional journalist and careful wordsmith.

George Anderson is a Long Island psychic who works in well-lighted rooms and live on radio and television.

Joel Martin and Patricia Romanowski, in *We Don't Die*, document his 85 to 90 percent accuracy in the face of consistent challenges from skeptics.

Mark Twain had it right: "Why *shouldn't* truth be stranger than fiction. Fiction, after all, has to make sense."

PRAYER

Prayer establishes a relation between God and man, a sense that both are part of the same universe.

In the Judeo-Christian tradition, God is seen as infinite, but also present in the world. He appears close when we reach out and distant when we do not. As Eliezer Berkovits explains it, we reach out in three ways: Driven by awe, we praise God. Driven by crisis, we ask salvation. Driven by salvation, we offer thanks.

The talmudic rabbis created a structure so that we could organize our prayers. We plan our communications carefully before asking someone to marry us or increase our salary; the rabbis believed that we should prepare so much more diligently before approaching the Supreme Being.

Judaism contains instances of communication with God. "Genesis" records that God told Adam not to eat fruit from two particular trees; when Adam and Eve ate anyway, God reproached and exiled them. Later in "Genesis," when God announced the destruction of Sodom and Gomorrah, Abraham replied, "Shall not the God of justice deal justly?" and bargained to save them if just ten virtuous men could be found living there. "Exodus" describes Moses' encounters with God at Midian and on Mt. Sinai. "Job" reports a conversation between God and its aging protagonist. The book of "Jonah" describes some sort of exchange between Jonah and God. The early conversations had some real give and take, but as the centuries pass the conversations become more implicit.

When Jesus of Nazareth walked the Earth, communication between God and humankind flourished as never before or since. During His public ministry, at least, the Gospels record that Jesus described the Godhead as triune, passed on to Peter the power to forgive sins, asked that the Eucharist be performed as His remembrance, and much more. From His words and deeds sprang the Christian churches in which a billion souls pray.

Jesus is described in the Gospels as praying often. Christians, related to the Father through Jesus as adopted children, are encouraged to pray regularly. The New Testament requirements are specific: unshakable confidence born of faith, perseverance, inner sincerity, and the loving fulfillment of God's commandments.

In modern times, we have little evidence of information transmission. Instead, as we transmit emotions to one another through music, we transmit emotions of praise, supplication, and thanks through prayer to God, and we receive emotions in return. God wants us to pray because He knows our souls need this nourishment.

Herman Wouk in *This is My God,* observes that language affects prayer. In Hebrew, the second tablet of the Ten Commandments reads something like, "Don't kill; don't be vile; don't steal, don't tell lies about others, don't envy any man his wife or house or animals, or anything he has." The genius of Hebrew is in its power to communicate magnificent ideas in a relaxed, colloquial style. When Jews pray in Hebrew there is a sense of intimacy with God.

As soon as you translate the Old Testament into English, a more distant eloquence appears. The King James Version presents the second tablet in what Wouk calls the grand, slow march of Thou Shalt Nots. The genius of English shows in its ability to convey religion in words with the formal beauty of stained glass windows.

GOD AND PHYSICS

Tradition has it that God is in heaven. The Judeo-Christian heritage informs us that God is everywhere, which leads to the possibility that heaven is the parallel universe in a different dimension. From that we might speculate that our universe is probably used for soul development, as part of a larger design. If so, we are born, as Wordsworth believed, trailing clouds of glory. Our souls are placed in delicate, perishable containers called "bodies," as wine is placed in wooden barrels, to mature. When the process is complete, the soul is said to "pass on"; perhaps Jacob's ladder is a metaphor for transubstantiation.

In the entire Judeo-Christian heritage, however, there appears to be no discussion of the mechanism by which we communicate with God. If He is everywhere, even in a different dimension, then He is inside our minds and can read, and write to, the electrochemical process that forms our thoughts. On this one humankind must retreat to the subordinate position. When two entities are greatly disproportionate in communication skills, the one with the greater skill does most of the work. Paul Tillich affirmed this point in *The New Being:* "We cannot bridge the gap between God and ourselves through the most intensive and frequent prayers. The gap between God and ourselves can only be bridged by God."

Chapter 10

OTHER LIFE FORMS

ON EARTH

We have barely begun to explore serious communication with the other senior species on our own planet. The historian Josephus informs us, in his *Antiquities of the Jews,* that Adam and Eve, after eating fruit from the Tree of Knowledge, lost the ability to talk with animals. Quite so. As the race that descended from the trees to become man evolved new forms of communication, it gradually lost the old ones.

On land, probably only the three great apes—the chimpanzees, gorillas, and orangutans—offer potential for communicating with humans. Since apes do not have vocal mechanics similar to our own, gesture and symbolic languages have proven the most effective methods. Washoe, a chimpanzee at the Institute of Primate Studies in Oklahoma, signs fluently in Ameslan. She can express original ideas, ask questions, and create new signs that humans are likely to understand. But expression is still

170

at a level like, "You tickle me." Washoe, Lucy, Koko, and the other communicating apes can tell us enough to interest the zoologist, but not the philosopher.

The sea is a more fertile environment for intelligent life forms. The great cetaceans—dolphins, porpoises, and whales—are the kings of the sea. Biologists call them "re-entrants," since their synapsid ancestors once lived on the land, and they are still air-breathing mammals.

The cetacean brain is strikingly similar to the human brain, but larger and more complex. It has extensive areas of cerebral cortex called "silent areas," larger than ours, which in humans are believed to handle creative intelligence, such as for long-range planning. Dr. John Lilly, the well-known marine biologist and pioneer of interspecies communication, believes that cetaceans are distinctly more intelligent than humans.

So far, humans and cetaceans have not talked much because our primary mode of conversation is designed for use in air while theirs is set up for use in water, a problem that even modern technology has only partly overcome. The stories about dolphins in particular, however, are startling in their cumulative impact. We hear of dolphins approaching humans and teaching them games to play in the water, saving humans from drowning, or guiding boats through rocky channels.

Apparently, cetaceans can process information a lot faster than we can. The human voice bandwidth runs about three kilohertz, and estimates are that we can comprehend at about four times the rate of speech. The cetacean's voice bandwidth is over one hundred kilohertz.

A conservative estimate, that the cetacean's audio bandwidth utilizes all of its information processing ability, would still mean the cetacean communicates and comprehends information at a rate eight to ten times faster than man. Apparently, this estimate works out in practice; researchers playing back dolphin recordings at greatly reduced speed have heard mimicries of human voices saying particular words the dolphin has heard before.

English, we say, has an insouciant way of picking up new words. So, perhaps, does Delphinese. In any event, dolphin conversations are highly specific. A clapping noise is a warning. A short whistle followed by a second high-pitched whistle is a distress signal. Rasping accompanied by the grating sound of dolphin sonar indicates searching, otherwise it is a feeding sound. Yelping is a mating signal. Dolphins also chirp, grunt, squeal, snort, click, make "bulb horn" sounds, and mimic the human voice. Each of these sounds has a whole range of specific variants; a scientist at Marineland of the Pacific recorded eleven hundred dolphin whistles and found only eighteen alike.

Plutarch wrote of the dolphin two thousand years ago: "Though it has no need at all of any man, yet it is a genial friend to all and has helped many." A serious conversation with a dolphin would be interesting. Dolphins are invariably friendly and helpful toward other dolphins, a rare characteristic among the higher land animals. What moral code do dolphins follow that allows them to attack sharks but prohibits them from attacking humans even under extreme provocation? Do cetacean societies practice Judeo-Christian ethics? Did the Christ ever come as a cetacean?

OUT THERE

If we encounter a civilization capable of interstellar communication, its denizens are apt to be of any conceivable size, shape, physical appearance, composition, or time scale, but there will be some constants. They are apt to live in organized societies as we do for their mutual benefit. They are likely to hold cooperation as a higher value than domination, because a house divided against itself cannot stand very long, and neither can a highly interdependent planet. They are also apt to have very advanced technology; humanlike creatures have walked around upright for a million years, yet we went from the horse and buggy to the moon in the same century. If another civilization reached the tipping point a slim thousand years before we did, it would already have solved problems that haven't even occurred to us yet.

We might be close to finding another civilization. Primitive life forms might exist on some of the moons of Jupiter and Saturn. More than forty nearby stars are surrounded by material in the early stages of becoming planets, which could result in environments that could nurture life. We might find more than "a civilization." Our Milky Way galaxy alone contains about 300 billion stars, and our nearest neighbor galaxy, Andromeda, contains 200 billion more. And there are said to be 100 billion other galaxies in the universe. Even if only one in a million stars has planets capable of supporting life, and only one in a million of those has an advanced civilization, there would still be an interstellar community of several hundred worlds and an intergalactic community of billions. It could be that in some far distant database, our Earth is a record marked: Pre-Emergent.

The Carrier

A carrier of interstellar communication would have to be easily distinguishable from natural static. It should resist absorption by space dust along its way or by a planet's atmosphere on its arrival. And it should move as fast as possible; Pioneer 10 and 11, and Voyager 1 and 2 are on their way but will not reach any other stars for tens of thousands of years. In fact, Pioneer 10, traveling toward the center of our galaxy at seven miles per second, will take about 200 million years to reach it.

Electromagnetic radiation as a communication carrier is the clear winner with today's technology. It travels at 186,000 miles per second, the fastest medium we have. Depending on its wave length, it can be either in the form of radio waves, light waves, X rays, or gamma rays. Man's technology has already made Earth the most powerful radio source in the solar system, more powerful even than the sun!

Microwave radio signals are the best kind of electro-magnetic radiation for interstellar communication. The universe produces relatively little radio energy; most of its natural radiation is at light, X ray, and gamma ray wave lengths. Wave lengths longer than about thirty centimeters have to compete with noise radiated by the Milky Way galaxy. Wave lengths shorter than about two centimeters compete with the hiss of atomic emissions. But microwave signals between three and thirty centimeters compete only with the background radiation left over from the creation, and after 15 billion years, that is fairly negligible. Better yet, microwaves in that one-to-ten-gigahertz range pass easily through the Earth's atmosphere.

If the life out there is water based, as Earth's is, it might notice that the natural radiation, or "spectral line," of neutral hydrogen is twenty-one centimeters. The natural radiation of the hydroxyl radical is eighteen centimeters. Both are right in the narrow three-to-thirty-centimeter window. Put them together and they form water. A 1972 government project on extraterrestrial intelligence put it this way: "[These two wave lengths] beckon all water-based life to search for their own kind at the age-old meeting place of all species: the water hole."

The challenge of communicating with a distant civilization will be formidable. Electromagnetic radio waves travel at the speed of light; it takes them four years to reach the nearest star and 30,000 years to reach the center of our own galaxy. It would then take as much time again for an answer to be returned. We either will need a medium faster than light or a reincarnation-based immortality to surmount this obstacle.

It may be that tachyons, subatomic particles that travel faster than light, could be used as carriers for interstellar communication. Physicists *think* tachyons exist. If so, they are the best bet on the horizon. For all we know, distant civilizations are sending tachyon signals to us right now, waiting for us to notice.

And the Code

All communication depends on a common base of experience; a signal is the analog of an idea shared by both sender and receiver. We have no way to anticipate the symbols used by extraterrestrial races. Scientists have suggested patterns based on the universal laws of physics or mathematics. Steven Spielberg used musical tones in *Close Encounters of the Third Kind*. The time delay caused by the extreme distances means we are apt to be milennia working out the code symbols.

Astronomer Frank Drake has come up with a brilliant "cosmic greeting card" based on the binary mathematical language used by our computers. It is a string of 1,679 ones and zeros, or "bits." Probably after some analysis, alien scientists will realize that 1,679 is the product of two prime numbers, 73 and 23. If they rearrange the bits into 73 rows of 23 characters each, and then represent the ones by light-colored squares and the zeros by dark-colored squares, they will discover a vital series of patterns.

At the top, from right to left, are binary representations of our numbers one through ten. Below the numbers, additional binary numbers give the atomic numbers of hydrogen, carbon, nitrogen, oxygen, and phosphorus, the basic elements of life on Earth. Next level down, twelve blocks of binary digits give the chemical formulas of the building blocks of DNA, the key to life here. A helix winding through the middle of the picture also represents DNA, which appears in the shape of a double helix. Below the helix is the result of this chemistry, a human, represented by a stick figure. Next to the figure on one side is a binary number representing the current population of the Earth; on the other are binary numbers representing human height, expressed as a multiple of the wave length used to send the message. Below the stick figure are a sun and nine planets, each in rough proportion to its actual size. The third planet, slightly raised, appears directly below the stick figure—an alien astronomer could deduce that the human comes from the third planet in a solar system whose planets are in that order of mass. The bottom is a picture of the radiotelescope at Arecibo, Puerto Rico, used to transmit the cosmic greeting card, together with its diameter in binary code.

Frank Drake transmitted his cosmic greeting card from Arecibo back in 1975. It has already passed the nearest stars!

Visiting with Extraterrestrials

The vast distances involved in interstellar travel have inspired science fiction writers to envision great arks, space colonies driven by fusion, whose passengers live and die in the ship over many generations. The more recent trend has been suspended animation, in which human metabolism is slowed almost to the vanishing point. The ship itself, smaller and virtually silent, would accelerate nearly to the speed of light, slowing down time itself on board so the sleeping passengers would age still more slowly, maybe over thousands of Earth years. Just before landing, automatic systems would awaken the still-young pioneers in time for their great adventure.

Travel in suspended animation is risky. Any of the ship's systems—propulsion, navigation, life support, or communication—could fail, leaving the whole expedition marooned or worse, with the Earth not even knowing about it for hundreds of years until the radio signals stopped.

There is another way. Taking Frank Drake's cosmic greeting card a long step further, we could transmit radio signals carrying complete digital models of terrestrial life, including the physical and cultural environment required for its survival. These "cybernetic seeds" could be used by advanced alien species to replicate human beings complete with memory and information.

Even in this transfer there are risks. True, a radio wave can travel at the speed of light for indefinite distances without equipment malfunctions. But suppose the advanced species regards its new arrivals as pets rather than ambassadors, or worse yet, as tasty snacks. A highly technical and emotionless alien species might alter the genetic codes for experimental reasons, creating bizarre versions and studying them in the laboratory. But there could be commensurate rewards; the advanced species is more apt to have a highly developed sense of morality and compassion and could share any secrets of immortality and omniscience both with the replicated "travelers" and with their cohorts on Earth.

Can we really consider this transmission "travel"? Probably as much as the old space ark passengers would have. In both cases, it is the genetic code itself, not any actual protoplasm, that survives the journey.

From one perspective, we ourselves are "space ships," or perhaps "time ships." Some philosophers say the master species on Earth is actually the genetic code, the double helix itself, that it has created men and women for the express purpose of its own immortality. The genetic codes, from this viewpoint, direct the construction of human beings as living environments. The codes allow these big, lumbering creatures to pursue any interests they want, but reserve assurance of their own survival by writing in powerful sex drives. When sperm unites with egg, the double helix leaps from an aging "house" to a brand new one, assuring that it will live forever.

Perhaps we won't need a radical breakthrough to meet alien beings. Traditionally, the higher intelligence does most of the work in an effort at communication. Perhaps they will use some sort of tachyon or black hole technology to come here, bypassing the delays inherent in wave propagation at the speed of light. They might talk to us directly by telepathy.

There is some reason to believe we have already been visited. Erich Von Däniken suggested that some 10,000 years ago, a race of Promethean astronauts came to Earth and imparted knowledge of metal making, agriculture, writing, and astronomy. Von Däniken's book, *Chariots of the Gods?*, was rife with errors but sold an astonishing 40 million copies over the years; apparently many people felt he was on to something.

The Great Pyramid at Giza, for instance, is built of 2.3 million blocks of rectangular limestone. Each block weighs an average of 2.5 tons. The pyramid's smooth sides rise at a uniform angle of fifty-one degrees, and the individual blocks are so well fitted together that a sharp knife blade cannot be inserted into the mortarless seams. The Greek historian Herodotus wrote that the construction occupied 100,000 men for twenty years. More interesting, it would take a modern computer quite a while to calculate the dimensions of each block to that level of precision!

Stonehenge is an earth shrine in southern England built by neolithic farmers more than forty centuries ago. Although at first glance it looks like a desolate pile of rocks, astronomers have found that practically every stone was placed to provide sights for the rising and setting of the sun on key dates, for instance, the summer and winter solstices. The fifty-six holes just inside the perimeter of the outer bank might have been used to track the moon and to predict lunar eclipses. This observatory shows knowledge of mathematics and astronomy.

After a million years of slow human progress, the sudden development of metal tools, the Neolithic Revolution, the advance of writing, the pyramid at Giza, the Stonehenge earth shrine, and other artifacts that demonstrate extraordinary new skills, invite inquiry into the origin of these skills. The sixth century B.C. manifests another leap of human creative energy, this time in Europe, Asia, and North America, all at the same time in separate civilizations. Our own century has been startling in its progress. In 1903 the Wright brothers tried a strange contraption at Kitty Hawk; within the span of a single human lifetime thereafter, Neil Armstrong walked on the moon. The race of Promethean astronauts might have chosen not to appear openly, but could account for much that we do not understand.

Most of the search for extraterrestrial intelligence is done by the Soviets. The United States' delay in pursuing extraterrestrial research is short sighted. The one-to-ten-gigahertz (three to thirty centimeter) radio range so valuable to space researchers is rapidly being occupied by mountaintop-to-mountaintop microwave telecommunication installations, satellite relays, even police radar and microwave ovens. As this background noise increases, it becomes more and more difficult to hear the faint signals researchers are looking for. Soon we will either have to move all our telecommunication networks off the one-to-ten-gigahertz range or set up a listening station on the far side of the moon.

The delay also reveals a narrow utilitarianism, a preoccupation with only the material side of the human experience. "Allow not nature more than nature needs," King Lear observed, "man's life is cheap as beast's." Every civilized government serves the spiritual side of the human experience with subsidies for great concerts and art museums. We all have felt the excitement of meeting an attractive stranger of the opposite sex; there is an exhilarating sense of challenge, of adventure. Imagine how much greater an adventure it would be to share with a new civilization what Bertrand Russell called "cosmic loneliness."

There is a third reason for us to move ahead quickly with the search for extraterrestrial intelligence. The intensity of the Soviet effort means that other civilizations will see the Earth through Soviet eyes, as a Soviet world.

Chapter 11

THE FUTURE

As we drift along in time, three areas are of enduring interest: electronic communication, organic communication, and interstellar communication.

In the next ten years, cellular and digital technology will transform our personal electronic communication systems. Most cars will be equipped with cellular telephones, and most Americans will own at least one cellular portable phone. Telephone numbers will be assigned to persons, rather than to lines as at present, so we will be able to reach and be reached wherever we go. The integrated services digital network will provide information and allow financial transactions on demand from vast data banks or financial banks, respectively, wherever we go.

Military research into parapsychology will continue. Perhaps both the United States and the Soviet Union will be impressed with the possibilities of secure, worldwide communication without equipment, without the need for the electromagnetic radio spectrum. Research into communication with other denizens of the galaxy will pick up in the next decade as advancing technology opens up new opportunities.

By a hundred years into the future, the challenges of electromagnetic communication will have been mostly solved. Geosynchronous satellites will make Saturnlike rings around the Earth and provide worldwide voice and data communication from anywhere to anywhere by means of small, wrist watchlike radios operating through cellular repeater systems.

By then, however, electromagnetic communication will be seen as having limits. No matter how small and sophisticated we make our transceivers, no matter how many communications cells we put up, it will all still be serial communication. If the sum of human knowledge continues to double every decade, it will be perhaps one thousand times the present body of knowledge by the end of the next century. Our progeny will be looking for a method of transmitting whole information structures at once.

As the limits of electronic technology emerge, military parapsychology research will spin off organic technology for communication. Organic technology is potent; nature can cram a lot more random-access memory into three pounds of human brain than humankind can into three pounds of electronic circuitry. In the next century, we will conduct enough research to arrive at replicable experiments; the odor of quark in the laboratory will be replaced by an exhilarating sense of a new frontier.

Interstellar communication in the next century will still be primitive. We will have isolated electronic signals generated by an intelligent civilization, but they will be so different from our own that we will have to work on a basic code. We will transmit, and perhaps receive, chemical formulas, representations of our solar system, and the like. Even so, conventional electromagnetic communication might still be limited to the speed of light; a single exchange would take centuries.

During the next milennium, organic communication will become so reliable that the electronic crutches will become antiquated. The cellular repeaters will be taken down; the geosynchronous satellite repeaters will be shut down. A person wanting to contact someone else will have only to think about communication, using standard techniques, and the link will form. By this time, the technique will be so refined that each of us will participate in the consciousness of all. John Donne's words, and the oneness of information sharing, will have come literally true. We will be one creature: humankind.

This oneness will still allow for privacy. Today, we sit in Lincoln Center and listen to Beethoven's Ninth Symphony. We know the way to get to our house, what is waiting for us at the office Monday morning, and a thousand other facts. We see three thousand other people in the audience. But on this night, we will not think of them. We abandon ourselves to the joyful chorus, *Freude schöner Gotterfunken Tochter aus Elysium.* In just this way will we, in the day when Beethoven's Ninth is an anthem, concentrate on the person we love, the person we are doing business with, the person with whom we are sharing experience.

The Bible passage that man was created in God's image will then be seen as the first prophecy. Early theologians read into that passage the idea of an anthropo*morphic* God, with head, torso, arms, and legs. That idea will be seen as a superfice; the reference was to an anthropo*sapient* God, reflected in a single living entity composed of billions of human cells, each nearly omniscient and omnipotent. Even now each human, a tiny reflection of God's image, is composed of billions of cells, each cell a repository of the whole genetic code.

Oneness will probably be the key to interstellar communication. Direct thought transfer might allow us to communicate with other civilizations as we do with one another.

A million years from now, the sounds in the forest will still be calls of birds and sighing wind in the trees, but we will hear an incredible profusion of voices. The oneness, the first prophecy, will include not only Earth but creatures of every kind from all over the galaxy. The world will stand out on either side so wide that our progeny will look back and say ours was a primitive civilization.

Five billion years from now, the sun will become a red giant star and immolate the Earth. By then, humankind will long since have journeyed on. In 100 trillion years, all the stars will lose their fuel, and the universe will grow dark and cold. Surviving creatures will live in artificially fueled, underground worlds and communicate with extreme efficiency in this era of scarce energy.

In an unimaginably distant time after that, even stable particles like protons will decay into lighter subnuclear particles. The long history of communication will end. The whole universe will be a few bits of dust scattered in eternity. From ashes to ashes, said Koheleth, from dust to dust.

Selected Bibliography

A book that ranges so widely over the landscape imposes a special challenge in source selection. The more than one hundred references listed below were winnowed from nearly one thousand available at the Library of Congress in Washington, D.C., where the primary research was done. I have included only those source books that are lively and interesting to the educated reader. Also, each book included here had to be current. Classic works of permanent value were consulted where the body of knowledge changes slowly, for instance, world history. Where current research is sparse, as in human pheromone communication, even material a decade or more old must be considered. At the opposite extreme, the organization of the telecommunications industry changed so dramatically in the mid-1980s that anything written before 1985 is of limited value. The books are arranged below in alphabetical order.

Abrams, Kathleen S. *Communication at Work.*
Englewood Cliffs, NJ: Prentice-Hall, 1986.

Adler, Ronald Brian. *Understanding Human Communication.*
New York: Holt, Rinehart, & Winston, 1985.

Barker, Larry Lee. *Communication.*
Englewood Cliffs, NJ: Prentice-Hall, 1987.

Baron, Dennis E. *Grammar and Gender.*
New Haven: Yale University Press, 1986.

Barron, John. *Breaking the Ring.*
Boston: Houghton Mifflin, 1987.

Berkovits, Eliezer. *Studies in Torah Judaism Prayer.*
New York: Yeshiva University, 1962.

Binder, Michael B. *Videotex and Teletext.*
Greenwich, CT: Jai Press, 1985.

Bittner, John R. *Fundamentals of Communication.*
Englewood Cliffs, NJ: Prentice-Hall, 1985.

Bixler, Susan. *The Professional Image.*
New York: Putnam, 1984.

Boase, Leonard. *The Prayer of Faith.*
Chicago: Loyola University Press, 1985.

Bonham, Frank. *Premonitions.*
New York: Holt, Rinehart, & Winston, 1984.

Brown, Rosemary. *Immortals by My Side.*
Chicago: H. Regnery Co, 1975.

Brown, Rosemary. *Unfinished Symphonies.*
New York: William Morrow, 1971.

Bruce, Robert R. *From Telecommunications to Electronic Services.*
Boston: Butterworths, 1986.

Buber, Martin. *I and Thou.*
New York: Charles Scribner's Sons, 1958.

Burton, Bob. *Top Secret.*
Boulder, CO: Paladin Press, 1986.

Cameron, Deborah. *Feminism and Linguistic Theory.*
New York: St. Martin's Press, 1985.

Cherwitz, Richard A. *Communication and Knowledge.*
Columbia, SC: University of South Carolina Press, 1986.

Comfort, A. "Likelihood of Human Pheromones."
Nature 230 (16 April, 1971): 432.

Conrad, Charles. *Strategic Organizational Communication.*
New York: Holt, Rinehart, & Winston, 1985.

Cook, William J. *Teleshock.*
New York: Pocket Books, 1985.

Corson, William R. *The New KGB, Engine of Soviet Power.*
New York: Quill, 1986.

Cox, Wesley. *Kiss Ma Bell Good-Bye.*
New York: Crown Publishers, 1985.

DeVito, Joseph A. *Human Communication.*
New York: Harper & Row, 1985.

Dizard, Wilson. *The Coming Information Age.*
New York: Longman, 1985.

Donin, Hayim. *To Be a Jew.*
New York: Basic Books, 1972.

Ellis, Andrew W. *The Psychology of Language and Communication.*
New York: Guilford Press, 1986.

Ellul, Jacques. *Prayer and Modern Man.*
New York: Seabury Press, 1970.

Fabre, Maurice. *A History of Communications.*
New York: Hawthorn Books, 1963.

Farb, Peter, and George Armelagos. *Consuming Passions: The Anthropology of Eating.*
New York: Washington Square Press, 1980.

Fast, Julius. *Body Language of Sex, Power, and Aggression.*
New York: M. Evans, 1977.

Finn, Stephen M. *Professional Persuasion.*
Woburn, MA: Butterworths, 1983.

Fisher, B. Aubrey. *Interpersonal Communication.*
New York: Random House, 1987.

Gibbins, Peter. *Particles and Paradoxes.*
Cambridge: Cambridge University Press, 1987.

Giblin, James. *From Hand to Mouth.*
New York: Crowell, 1987.

Golden, Nancy. *Dress Right for Business.*
New York: Gregg Div., McGraw-Hill Book Co., 1986.

Gordon, George N. *Erotic Communications.*
New York: Hastings House, 1980.

Hamman, Adalbert. *Prayer; The New Testament.*
Chicago: Franciscan Herald Press, 1971.

Haney, William V. *Communication and Interpersonal Relations.*
Homewood, IL: Irwin, 1986.

Haslett, Beth. *Communication, Strategic Action in Context.*
Hillsdale, NJ: L. Erlbaum Associates, 1987.

Hawkins, Gerald. *Mindsteps to the Cosmos.*
New York: Harper & Row, 1983.

Hawkins, Gerald. *Stonehenge Decoded.*
Garden City, NY: Doubleday, 1965.

Hertz, David M. *The Tuning of the Word.*
Carbondale, IL: Southern Illinois University Press, 1987.

Hewitt, Roger. *White Talk Black Talk.*
Cambridge: Cambridge University Press, 1986.

Hoemann, Harry W. *Introduction to American Sign Language.*
Bowling Green, OH: Bowling Green Press, 1986.

Hopson, Janet L. "Scent and Human Behavior: Olfaction or Fiction?"
Science News 115 (28 April, 1979): 282-283

Jameson, G. Harry. *Communication and Persuasion.*
London: Croom Helm, 1985.

Johnson, Lee McKay. *The Metaphor of Painting.*
Ann Arbor, MI: UMI Research Press, 1980.

Kaiser, Susan B. *Social Psychology of Clothing and Personal Adornment.*
New York: Macmillan, 1985.

Kalin, Martin J. *Telecommunications Policies in Ten Countries.*
Washington, DC: Dept. of Commerce (U.S.G.P.O.), 1985.

Kittler, Glenn D. *Edgar Cayce on the Dead Sea Scrolls.*
New York: Paperback Library, 1970.

Knightley, Phillip. *The Second Oldest Profession.*
New York: Norton, 1987.

Koestler, Arthur. *The Ghost in the Machine.*
London: Hutchinson, 1967.

Koestler, Arthur. *The Roots of Coincidence.*
London: Hutchinson, 1972.

Kübler-Ross, Elisabeth. *Living with Death and Dying.*
New York: Collier Books, 1984.

Lamb, Warren. *Body Code.*
London: Routledge & Kegan Paul, 1979.

Lilly, John C. *Communication Between Man and Dolphin.*
New York: Julian Press, 1987.

Linkemer, Bobbi. *Polishing Your Professional Image.*
New York: American Management Association, 1987.

Littlejohn, Stephen W. *Persuasive Transactions.*
Glenview, IL: Scott, Foresman, 1987.

Luciani, V.J. *Amateur Radio, Super Hobby.*
New York: McGraw-Hill, 1984.

Mallery, Garrick. *Sign Language Among North American Indians.*
The Hague: Mouton, 1972.

Martin, Joel, and Patricia Romanowski, *We Don't Die.*
New York: Putnam, 1988

Maurer, Evan M. *The Native American Heritage.*
Chicago: The Institute, 1977.

McClintock, Martha K. "Menstrual Synchrony and Suppression"
Nature 229 (22 January, 1971): 244.

McGinnis, Lila Sprague. *Auras and Other Rainbow Secrets.*
New York: Hastings House, 1984.

McLaughlin, Terence. *Music and Communication.*
New York: St. Martin's Press, 1971.

Moody, Raymond A. *Life after Life.*
Harrisburg, PA: Stackpole Books, 1976.

Moody, Raymond A. *Reflections on Life After Life.*
Harrisburg, PA: Stackpole Books, 1977.

Moyne, John A. *Understanding Language.*
New York: Plenum Press, 1985.

Neubauer, John. *The Emancipation of Music from Language.*
New Haven: Yale University Press, 1986.

Ortega y Gasset, José. *El Hombre y La Gente.*
Madrid: Revista de Occidente, 1980.

Pante, Robert. *Dressing to Win.*
Garden City, NY: Doubleday, 1984.

Pateman, Trevor. *Language in Mind and Language in Society.*
Oxford, UK: Clarendon Press, 1987.

Pearson, Judy C. *Gender and Communication.*
Dubuque, IA: W. C. Brown Publishers, 1985.

Petty, Richard E. *Communication and Persuasion.*
New York: Springer-Verlag, 1986.

Polanyi, Michael. *Meaning.*
Chicago: University of Chicago Press, 1975.

Prosch, Harry. *Michael Polanyi: A Critical Exposition.*
Albany, NY: State University of New York Press, 1986.

Rae, Alastair I. M. *Quantum Physics, Illusion or Reality.*
Cambridge: Cambridge University Press, 1986.

Reardon, Kathleen K. *Interpersonal Communication.*
Belmont, CA: Wadsworth, 1987.

Regush, Nicholas M. *Exploring the Human Aura.*
Englewood Cliffs, NJ: Prentice-Hall, 1975.

Richmond, Virginia P. *Communication.*
Scottsdale, AZ: Gorsuch Scarisbrick, 1985.

Riekehof, Lottie L. *The Joy of Signing.*
Springfield, MO: Gospel Publishing House, 1978.

Russell, Bertrand. *A History of Western Philosophy.*
New York: Simon & Schuster, 1945.

Rutter, Derek R. *Communicating by Telephone.*
New York: Pergamon Press, 1987.

Sagan, Carl. *Contact.*
New York: Simon & Schuster, 1985.

Sagan, Carl. *Cosmos.*
New York: Random House, 1980.

St. Johns, Adela Rogers, *No Good-Byes.*
New York: McGraw-Hill, 1981.

Sandager, Oliver K. *Sign Languages Around the World.*
North Hollywood, CA: OK Publishers, 1986.

Sarles, Harvey B. *Language and Human Nature.*
Minneapolis: University of Minnesota Press, 1985.

Schwartz, Gary E. *Proceedings of Yale Conference on Behavioral Medicine.*
New Haven, CT: U.S. National Institutes of Health, 1977.

Sharpe, Deborah T. *The Psychology of Color and Design.*
Chicago: Nelson-Hall Co., 1974.

Sheldrake, Rupert. *A New Science of Life.*
Los Angeles: J. P. Tarcher, 1981.

Sherman, Barry L. *Telecommunications Management.*
New York: McGraw-Hill, 1987.

Sherman, Harold M. *Extra Success Potential.*
Englewood Cliffs, NJ: Prentice-Hall, 1981.

Simon, Sam. *After Divestiture.*
White Plains, NY: Knowledge Industry Publications, 1985.

Stanford, Ray. *What Your Aura Tells Me.*
Garden City, NY: Doubleday, 1977.

Sugarman, Joan G. *Inside the Synagogue.*
New York: Union of American Hebrew Congregations, 1984.

Swann, Ingo. *How to Develop Your ESP.*
Toronto: Bantam Books, 1987.

Talbot, Michael. *Beyond the Quantum.*
New York: Macmillan, 1986.

Tannen, Deborah. *That's Not What I Meant!*
New York: Morrow, 1986.

Tillich, Paul. *The New Being.*
New York: Scribner, 1955.

Trenholm, Sarah. *Human Communication Theory.*
Englewood Cliffs, NJ: Prentice-Hall, 1986.

Tubbs, Stewart L. *Human Communication.*
New York: Random House, 1986.

Tunstall, Jeremy. *Communications Deregulation.*
Oxford, UK: B. Blackwell, 1986.

Van Loon, Hendrik Willem. *The Arts.*
New York: Simon & Schuster, 1937.

Van Loon, Hendrik Willem. *The Story of Mankind.*
New York: Liveright, 1972.

Von Däniken, Erich. *Chariots of the Gods?*
New York: Putnam, 1974.

Weisman, Donald. *Language and Visual Form.*
Austin, TX: University Of Texas Press, 1968.

Wells, C. Gordon. *How to Communicate.*
London: McGraw-Hill, 1986.

Wiley, Terence G. *Communicating in the Real World.*
Englewood Cliffs, NJ: Prentice-Hall, 1987.

Williams, Joseph M. *Origins of the English Language.*
New York: Free Press, 1975.

Wood, Ananda E. *Knowledge Before Printing and After.*
New York: Oxford University Press, 1985.

Wouk, Herman. *This Is My God.*
New York: Touchstone Books, 1986.

Yule, George. *The Study of Language.*
Cambridge: Cambridge University Press, 1985.

INDEX

.

The Date Due Card in the pocket in-
dicates the date on or before which
this book should be returned to the
Library.
Please do not remove cards from this
pocket.